SKETCHES FROM SANTALISTAN

SKETCHES FROM SANTALISTAN

By

M.A. PEDERSON

GYAN

Published by

GYAN

Gyan Publishing House
5, Ansari Road
Daryaganj, New Delhi-110002
Phone: 011-47034999, 9811692060
E-mail: books@gyanbooks.com

Distribution Network
gyanbooks.com
India, USA, Canada, UK, Australia, France

ISBN : 978-81-212-6729-8 (PB)
First Published, 1913

2nd Impression 2022

Printed at: Gyan Press, Delhi.

SKETCHES FROM SANTALISTAN
Author: M. A. PEDERSON

Sketches from Santalistan.

By

M. A. Pederson,

Missionary.

1913.

KAERABANI CHURCH AND CONGREGATION.

FOREWORD.

The author of these sketches is not laboring under the illusion that this book has been looked for and expected for a long time, and that it now, at last, comes to fill a "long felt want." The world has gotten along so far without any "Sketches from Santalistan" and would likely manage to plod along to the end of time without even missing them. He has written them because he liked to write them.

These sketches have been written from time to time during a period of eight years and some of them have been published in various papers and rewritten for this volume. They are written especially for the young people in our Scandinavian Lutheran Churches, and not only for those young in years, but for everybody with a young heart.

The aim has been to bring a missionary's daily life and labors as well as the people among whom he works a little closer to the friends in the home-lands and, if possible, also to kindle a little more interest in the greatest of all causes, Missions.

M. A. P.

THE GATE OF INDIA.

The Indian ocean was dull. Dark and oily lay the waters with only a slight swell. There was no wind nor waves for it was October, and the monsoon was over. Slowly the hot days and even hotter nights crept by. On leaving Aden you begin to notice a change both in yourself and in others. The manners and customs of the West are being left behind and now, unconsiously perhaps, one begins to pick up the ways of the East.

Sedate and elderly gentlemen, whom you learned to know while in the Mediterranean as propriety incarnate, can now be seen walking the decks in the early mornings, barefoot and attired only in striped pajamas.

It is the spirit of the East. You fight against it to begin with. You swelter in the privacy of your cabin and count the bells till dawn, when you dress and get on deck. There you find your fellow passengers on their mattresses fast asleep, their bare feet sticking out from under their coverings, catching the sea-breeze, which gives them an air of cool comfort that you did not enjoy in your hot and stuffy cabin. Consequently, next evening you break with the traditions of the progressive West and fall into the ways of the strange and mysterious eastern world. You bring your mattress on deck, robe yourself for the night and go to sleep under the starlit eastern sky. Whether it is the languor of the tropics or the influence of the mysterious spirit of the East, you cannot tell, but you feel a sense of security and calm; a sort of homelike feeling takes posession of you as if you had at last come to your own. Fanned by the soft sea-breeze you close your eyes and doze and dream and rest. You are "east of Suez" and the East has conquered you. That mysterious world of which it is said that it is never quite awake by day and never quite asleep at night, has made you one of her own.

You watch the flying fishes skip the surface of the quiet water as the crimson curtains of the morning are drawn aside and the sun appears out of the sea, a great ball of yellow fire. It is your last day on shipboard. Before noon the hazy outlines of the mountains, known as the Ghats, can be traced through your fieldglass, and as the day declines your good ship is at anchor in the harbor of Bombay, the western gate of the Indian Empire.

On landing you fall headlong, as it were, into the lap of her, who has adopted you, the eastern world. It is a world entirely different from anything you have so far seen and experienced. You have nothing to compare it with. It feels like a dream, indescribable, wierd, and complex like the spinning dance of a Dervish.

Everything about you is now different; even the most common things are changed — different clothes, different food, different mealtimes. You begin to realize that you are called upon to begin a new life in this new world.

At first everything seems blurred and out of focus. You try to notice everything and you see nothing. You ask an assistant in the custom office to get a drayman to take your baggage to your hotel. He beckons to a chocolate colored, almost naked man squatting near by and gives him a command in a strange tongue. In a few moments the man returns, bringing up a ridiculous two-wheeled cart, drawn by a pair of small gray oxen, each with a funny looking hump on its shoulders, and short stubby horns painted a bright red.

Your room is on the second floor of the hotel. There are no windows in it, but many doors, the most of which lead out to the open veranda. As you sit down to try to gather your scattered wits and to get used to your surroundings, a crow, the color of blue steel, settles on the veranda railing, lays its head on one side, as if to inspect you, and when, as it seems, it has found you an object worthy of observation, it at once summons its compatriots to share in the new discovery. In a moment there is a dozen crows on the railing busy discussing you, your family, your baggage, and everything about you with the greatest impunity. You may try to drive them away, but they only move a foot or two, and their vociferous remarks grow more personal and impertinent.

As you watch them, you begin to remember what you have read about the transmigration of souls. While at home you put the idea aside as childish nonsense, but when you look at the crows and their impudent bearing, you must admit that you are filled with an uncanny feeling of doubt. Perhaps after all there is such a thing as transmigration, and that these little bodies are inhabited by the souls of Hindus, who in former existance earned the punishment of being reincarnated as crows.

You are taken to the bazaar. You pass down narrow and crooked lanes thronged with people attired in all kinds of strange garbs. The stores or shops, as they are called are only little stalls where the merchants sit tailor fashion with their goods laid out on the floor about them. And the dust, the smells, the clouds of flies and other insects, the shouting and vociferous jabbering of the people, the gorgeous mixture of colors, of silk and rags, — all go to make up a picture both strange and fascinating.

A drive to Malebar Hill in the cool of the evening you will never forget. The Parsees, sometimes called the Jews of the East, live there. The hill is one luxurious garden with beautiful bungalows, half hidden by tropical flowers and trees.

As you drive along, enjoying the sights, so strange and beautiful, your guide points out to you a low, round, roofless tower set in the middle of a large park gorgeous with blossoming trees, shrubs and creepers. It is the "Tower of Silence." To it the Parsees carry their dead and leave them to be devoured by vultures. And as you look you will notice that the tower is literally fringed with those birds of prey. They are perched there quietly waiting for their next meal.

The Tower and the repulsive idea connected with it sends a shudder through you. For the rest of the evening you see and enjoy nothing. Slowly the sun dips into the Indian ocean. All Bombay comes out for a promenade and a breath of sea-breeze along the beach. The sunset sky, the passing rows of beautiful vehicles and the people in their bright colored clothes, all go to make up a picture which would charm even the most weary globe-trotter, but you hardly see it. In vain you try to rid yourself of that repulsive picture of the gorged and sleepy vultures in that beautiful garden.

In time you will learn that even this is the "Spirit of

the East." In the midst of a beauty, almost supernatural, there is a vulture crowded "Tower of Silence," or a horrid something, standing out prominently, and unblushingly casting its dark shadow of horrors across this fairest scene. You can but turn to Him, who knows the inmost yearnings of your soul, and pray that you may be permitted to contribute your little mite towards the removal of all that, which mars the fair picture of the fair East.

MISSION CHURCH AT BENAGARIA.

SANTALISTAN.

Santalistan is not an official name. You will not find it on the map. The name is applied colloquially to the district in northern Bengal where the Santals live.

If you take a map of India and find Calcutta, the old capital of the Empire, you will notice that the river Ganges bends to the west about a hundred and fifty miles north of that city. This bend is generally called the elbow of the Ganges.

Santalistan is part of the country lying in the elbow of that famous river.

The official name of the main part of Santalistan is Santal Parganas. It has an area of about 4800 square miles and is nearly as large as the state of Connecticut.

The Santals are not, however, confined to this district, but are scattered about in northern Bengal and Assam. Neither are all the people in the Santal Paraganas Santals. A great number of the inhabitants are Hindus of the various castes and there are also a large number of Mohammedans.

In a certain sense the Santal Parganas has been set

aside for the Santals. Here they receive certain privileges from the government and are protected by special laws.

Santalistan is comparatively high and hilly. One might say, perhaps, that it consists of a number of rocky hills with stretches of prairie in between them. These hills are not very high. Lokhonpur hill, — the Santals call it a

THE VILLAGE POND.

mountain — has an elevation of but 2311 feet above sea level.

If you feel equal to the exertion and the day is not too hot it will pay you to climb it. There are goat paths leading up between the boulders. In some places the climb is very steep and you will wish you had as many legs as the pathmakers. The barefoot Santal boys, however, do not mind it in the least. They skip along like monkeys and pity your slow progress, evidently thinking, that you are very clumsy on a mountain path.

At last you have reached the top. You wipe the perspiration from your brow and look out upon the lovely panorama spread out before you. Glittering in the sunlight are brooks and rivers meandering through the valleys. It is early October and you can still see the water glistening in the dark green rice fields, and there are also patches of other crops, such as millet and pulse in various shades of color, making the plain appear like a great crazy-quilt spread out in the sun.

Here and there you get glimpses of the straw-thatched roofs or whitewashed walls of a village. It is a scene so full of peace and beauty that it captivates you. It is like a beautiful dream and you forget the fleeting hours. The sun is sinking. From the hillside below you the evening breeze wafts up to you the melancholy notes of a shepherd's flute as he wends his way homeward with his flock. A last lingering look and you come away enriched with memories that will remain with you as long as life. You have had a glimpse of a bit of Santalistan.

The hills are wooded to the very top. On the highest slopes one will find the hill-bamboo, tall, straight and graceful, its thin feathery leaves hanging fringe-like from its branches and quivering in the smallest breeze. There is the stately edel, or Indian cotton tree, and further down towards the foot you will find the tall and straight sarjon or sal, the sacred tree of the Santals. While scattered about on hillside and plain, among the rice fields and about the village grows the sturdy matkon tree. The flower of this tree is eaten by the people and is quite nourishing.

The Santals are clearers of land, diggers and grubbers. It seldom occurs to them to plant trees, but they cut them and clear them away. For that reason there is very little timber or jungle left in the Santal country. Only where protected by the forest department of the Government, patches of jungle remain. Of course, there are a few shade trees about the villages; otherwise, compared to other parts of India the country must be said to be rather treeless.

The soil is sandy and rather poor compared with the rich alluvial of the Gangetic plain; but if it receives sufficient rain will produce good crops. The lowlands or valleys are made into rice fields, while the higher land yields corn, small grain and oilseeds. Some land in each village is set aside for grazing purposes and there is very little waste land.

Coal is found in several places, but in the Santal Parganas it is of a rather inferior quality and very little use is found for it. Iron ore is found quite abundantly, and there are also traces of other metals, such as lead and mica.

About the climate of Santalistan you will be able to form an idea when you learn that it lies about as far north of the equator as the island of Cuba.

LEARNING THE LANGUAGE.

You will soon discover that it is more work than play to learn a new language, when you are getting on in years, especially a language so intricate as Santali.

Very often you get discouraged. With twenty-seven tenses of the verb and many other intricacies entirely foreign to all your ideas of what language ought to be, you sometimes feel, that it is no use trying; you might as well give up first as last. But when you hear a little Santal boy, as yet not old enough for a loincloth, chattering away in Santali, as if it were the only language in the world, you take courage and push on anew. When that little boy could learn to speak Santali, why cannot you?

Santali is printed in Roman characters, which is a decided advantage for you. Most of the Indian languages are printed in characters of their own. And yet you will find that though you know the letters by sight you do not know them by sound. The first letter in the alphabet, for instance, has four distinct sounds, each indicated by diacritical marks. A few letters represent sounds peculiar to the Santal language, and these, a European can pronounce only after long and diligent practice.

First you get the rudiments of the grammar and some drilling in pronounciation; then you learn to say "Chet kana?" (what is that?) Armed with this magic phrase you go out into the villages among the people. You point at a tree and say: "Chet kana?"

Dignity must be thrown aside, you must take lessons from everybody. You have to play the natural role of an ignoramus running about asking for the names of the most common objects; and when you hear them and try to twist your tongue around those almost inhuman sounds you often fail most pathetically. But your efforts amuse the people. Many a hearty laugh they get at your expense. And they do not wait until you are out of the way, but laugh straight in your face. But you soon learn to laugh with them. So much, at least, you know, that laughing and crying is expressed in the same way the world over.

And all the blunders you will make! I am sure you would laugh yourself blue in the face if I told you some of mine, but I will not; I know how to keep secrets.

You struggle on with the few words and phrases you have learned and eke them out with profuse gestures until you manage to make yourself understood; and when the people find that you are in earnest about learning their language, they vie with one another in their efforts to help you on.

It is often dificult to get a good native teacher. The common fault of native teachers is that they try to explain things to you loquaciously and usually manage to get you so tangled up in their explanations that you get entirely bewildered. Women and children are the best teachers. They speak more slowly and as a rule, more distinctly than men, and, besides, they do not try to explain so much.

How glad you are, when you at last have got so far,

that you can carry on a simple conversation! Your courage grows by leaps and bounds. At last you feel that you can begin to speak a word for Him, whose name you have come to proclaim.

Then your first sermon! How well you prepare it, weigh every statement, and think that this sermon they will never forget. Great will be your surprise, when some one is honest enough to tell you, that he did not understand very much of what you said. Your choice of words and your pronounciation may, in the main, have been correct, but your way of thinking and presenting the truth is that of the West, and therefore foreign to your audience. Again off to school you must go. You have to put yourself at the feet of, perhaps, an old illiterate Santal and from him learn how to preach so, that the people may be able to understand you. This is a new field to be mastered and your college and seminary diploma will not help you much.

The Santal presents a new type of character, entirely different from what you are used to. His ways of looking at things are not your ways and his ideas are not your ideas. If you are to meet in sympathy you must lay aside your dignity of learning, if you have any, and get down to where he is and fall into his way of thinking and feeling. And that can be done only when you possess some of that love she had, who said to her mother-in-law: "Thy people shall be my people."

VILLAGE PREACHING.

Some good people in the homelands seem to think that the heathen are just dying for an opportunity to hear the gospel, and that they have been anxiously looking for an invitation to become Christians. But that is far from true. It is not true even of the ungodly masses at home. They are anxious neither to hear the Gospel nor to come to God. It is rather the other way. They try apparently to get as far away from God and the infulence of his word as posible. For this reason Christian workers at home have to go out into the streets and the highways, into the fields and shops, and preach to them in order that they may know the way of salvation.

If a missionary comes to the heathen with the idea that they are anxiously waiting for him to proclaim the good news to them, he will soon know his mistake. This is a land where the people for ages and ages have been bound by the superstitions of lidolatry, and have been taught to look with suspicion on everything foreign. Indeed they think they can get along very well without both the missionary and his preaching.

The heathen do not come to the missionary, he must

go to them. In our Santal field it is not very common that a non-christian comes to church. If he is to hear the gospel at all, it must be preached to him in his own village or home. There is where the work of the missionary begins.

Early in the morning, together with one or more catechists, the missionary will go aut to the villages. The pariah dogs will announce his arrival, and the children playing in the streets will shout "Saheb, Saheb!" This helps to advertise his meeting and bring out the people. Usually a bedstead is brought out into the street and he is asked to take a seat. He looks at the bed and if his suspicions are aroused be will take up as small a portion of it as possible. The village oilpress, or a flat stone under some spreading tree, also offers a convenient seat and a good gathering-place

Sometimes however, the missionary is not offered a seat at all, but asked to go and preach in the next village. Such cases, fortunately, are exceptions — in our district. As a rule, the people are polite and greet the Padre Saheb or missionary with cordial "johars" and invite him to be seated. Even though they do not care so much for what he has to say, they enjoy looking at him. Being white, he is a curiosity.

In a little while quite a crowd will gather. The missionary will ask all to sit down, and they squat on the ground — that is, the men and boys do. The women will remain standing at a distance.

The native Christian worker will then sing a song, usually gospel words fitted to some of the old Santal tunes. Then either the missionary or the cathechist will explain the song and invite the people to come to the Savior. After reading a few words of Scripture the missionary will begin to talk. It will not be preaching in the sense in which that word is used in the West. Preaching here is more in the form of a conversation. Everybody is at liberty to make remarks, and the more remarks made, the better.

Religious truth must be presented to them in such a form that they can grasp it. The missionary must have recourse to parables, pictures and illustrations taken from the lives of the people.

All sorts of objections against Christianity are raised and must be patiently met. And the speaker must not let himself be distracted if he should hear someone in the outskirts of the crowd making sundry remarks on his personal appearance, remarks very much like those a visitor at the zoo will make about the animal he is looking at.

One will very seldom now-a-days find a Santal, who will try to defend his "Bongas" or gods and his heathen worship. On the other hand it is often quite amusing to hear these people run down and ridicule their "Bongas." "They are a worthless lot," they will say, "that only do us harm, and as to helping us, they only help us to spend everything we have, so that our children often have to go naked and hungry."

"Well, why don't you leave them then?"

"That is not so easy" they will reply, "because our fathers have shown us this way and left us in the power of the "Bongas."

"Now see here, my friend; if your father had given you in service to a certain master, who treated you very cruelly, never gave you any pay and never offered you anything to eat or to wear, but on the contrary in every possible way caused you pain and suffering, would you keep on year after year serving such a master? Would you not run away from him? I think you would, if you looked to your own interests. And here is your real master, your Savior, calling you to come to him and rest. If you suffer, you have no one but yourself to blame; for Christ has been calling you, and is calling you again today."

Sometimes one will meet people who want to have an argument with the missionary. Little, however, is gained by arguing. The man, when beaten in argument, will get angry and leave in a huff and will most likely become an enemy, or else he will laugh and say, "I am no match for you in a discussion."

There are many things to which they can agree. Sin, sickness, death and sorrow they all know. They will always listen to the simple story how God has met our needs and opened a way back to himself for sinful man through Jesus Christ.

At these street meetings the seed is sown broadcast, as it were. In some heart, somewhere, some truth will lodge, which under God's care some day will bear fruit.

But in the missionfield, as everywhere else, for that matter, it is personal work that counts. Brother dealing with brother heart to heart. Sitting on the embankment between the ricefields with his single listener the preacher will tell the old, old story. At last the listener will say, "O yes, I am tired of the "Bongas.' Since my child died I have offered no sacrifices to them. And both my wife and I often talk about it, that we should like to become Christians. But you know it will be hard for us, as all our relatives and friends are heathen." This objection is overcome and the family is ready to recieve instruction. Then when the main truths of the Christian religion are mastered they are baptized.

VILLAGE SCHOOLS.

Schools are not the rule among the Santals, but rather the exception. Outside of the districts, in which there are Christians, who have taken the lead, there are very few distinctly Santal schools. The common Santal does not think it necessary to educate his children. His views on education are expressed in about the following terms: "Our fathers and grandfathers did not know how to read and write, we have not learned it, then why should our sons go to school and grow up to be idlers. Let them go into the fields and work, let them take care of the cattle and goats, then they can get something for their stomachs. You can not eat paper."

A few of the non-Christian Santals have however seen the advantage of an education and are sending their sons to some village school where they learn to read and write the Bengali language. An old village headman said; "It is a good thing to have one or two in the village able to read and write. When we get a summons from the court as witnesses or a letter is sent us, then our own boys can tell us what the paper says."

Apart from natural sluggishness the Hindu caste system is responsible for this state of affairs. For ages and ages the Brahmin has carried the burden of education for all classes. It was a deadly sin to educate a boy of a low birth; and as for educating women, that was entirely out of the question. But western influence and western law has

A VILLAGE SCHOOL.

changed all this. Schools are now scattered throughout the country, and an opportunity of acquiring an education is within the reach of every one, even the poorest Santal.

Let us take a peep at the typical Santal school.

You need not look for the school house, for there is none. The scholars squat in the village street or in the shade of a tree and the schoolmaster, stick in hand, is usually seated on a stool in their midst. If it is cold, he allows his school to find a sunny wall, where they are sheltered from the wind. The so-called Manjhithan also offers shade and shelter when that is needed.

But I must tell you what a Manjhithan is. It is an earth platform raised a foot or two above the ground. There are five posts, one at each corner and one in the center, supporting a thatched roof. Around the post in the center you will notice a few pebbles the size of an egg sticking out of the earth. In these pebbles the spirits of the departed village headmen dwell, one spirit in each pebble. Under this roof the villagers hold their councils and the spirits of the departed are supposed to aid them in their deliberations and lead them in the paths of wisdom.

When a boy is brought to school the first thing he has to learn, according to the opinion of the teacher, is to sit still. This is indeed a hard lesson for an active Santal boy, but through generous assistance of the master's stick the lesson is in time learned and he is ready for advancement. He is then given over to one of the bigger boys who traces a letter in the dust with his finger. This letter the beginner must retrace times without number, each time shouting out the name of that letter at the top of his voice. It is quite an entertainment to listen to dozen boys all at once "barking" away at the alphabet in this manner. It reminds one of a dog show.

The teacher will explain to us that this method has a great advantage besides that of being old, it teaches reading and writing at the same time. He might also add that it developes their lungs.

At last the boy gets a book. And a proud little fellow he is as he comes down the village street with his first book under his arm securely tied up in an old rag. He is on the highroad to learning. Now his work begins in earnest. He has to learn the letters by rote. A few days more of shouting and he will be able to read them off from beginning to end like a table. But if you take a leaf from the jackfruit

READY FOR SCHOOL.

tree close by, make a small hole in the center of it, put it on the page of his reader, and move it about so that he can see but one letter at the time, you will be surprised to find how many he misses. But give him plenty of time — and time is cheap in India — and he will eventually learn to read, write, and do sums on his slate, or on the ground and in his head.

It is but fair to state, however, that in the schools under the supervision of the government or the mission, the above described method is getting more and more obsolete. Western methods and text-books are bringing about a change for the better in the old Bengali school system. One thing you will not fail to notice in all the village schools, even the best and most up to date ones, and that is that all the studying is done by reading aloud, and the louder the better. A village school can be heard long before it is seen.

MODES OF TRAVEL.

There are two kinds of people in Santalistan, those who travel and those who do not. The travelers are again divided into two classes, those who travel afoot and those who do not.

Traveling afoot is pretty much the same all the world over. It seems to be man's natural way of locomotion, and is very likely, as old as the human race. In the West it is not popular any longer. No end of machinery and devices have been invented by ingenious men to do away with the old style of locomotion, but in the conservative East, where modes change but slowly it is a very common, if not altogether a popular, way of getting from one place to another.

On market days one can see long lines of foot passengers pass by in single file, some carrying their products away to be sold or exchanged, others carrying nothing but their sticks. Or if you are near some of the great highways you can often see pilgrims by the half hundred trudging wearily along on their way to some shrine. But we are not concerned with them. It is those who do not travel afoot we are interested in just now.

Bicycles are not very common. Some few years ago they were a great curiosity in the eyes of the natives. I well remember that once a fellow-worker and I were out on a tour. He had a bicycle and I rode a horse. While passing from one mission center to another we took what we thought would be a short cut through the jungle. As we passed through a Santal village some children at play

CROSSING A STREAM.

in the street saw us and set up an alarm. At once the whole male population of the village turned out and pursued the cyclist. Had I not known that they were moved by curiousity, I should have been alarmed at seeing some twenty Santals racing along at top speed chasing after a missionary.

Some Santals were one day standing about a bicycle and discussing the question how is was possible for a person to stay on it without the whole thing upsetting. This phenomenon one man undertook to explain in the following way: "You see, it's like this, it's the wind that does everything. A bicycle is like a railway engine, except that a bicycle is run by wind and an engine by steam. I have seen the Saheb every dag, before he starts out, pumping wind into the wheels to make them go. If there is no wind in the wheels they will not go."

Horseback riding is quite common, and has the great advantage that one can with a good horse get over nearly all kinds of roads and even across country where there are no roads at all. The best horses are imported from Australia. They are called Walers. But they are costly. As a rule a missionary is not overburdened with a great deal of this world's goods and therefore cannot buy costly horses. He must generally be contented with a so-called "country tat," that is, a country-bred pony. I possessed one of these animals once. It cost me twenty dollars and the saddle cost twenty-two. Only by courtesy could it be called a horse. It answered literally to a soldier's definition of a government mule: "An animal which bites at one end and kicks at the other and is extremely uncomfortable in the middle." On various commonplace and practical subjects my "tat" held extremely advanced opinions which no amount of persuasion or argument could shake. At last however, we got to understand one another, and, by avoiding subjects about which we knew we could not agree, we managed to get along quite well.

Some people have what they call a "tomtom," a two-wheeled cart or gig for one horse. But the trouble is that in order to get about with those, one must have roads. And

so long as roadmaking and roadrepairing is as unpopular among the Santal villagers as it is at the present time, a vehicle of that sort will not be of much use. Where one has access to the roads built and repaired by the government, the case is different.

The tika ghari" is a four wheeled carriage, in appear-

THE TIKA GHARI.

ance not unlike a Chicago milk delivery wagon, only much heavier and clumsier. Perhaps you would get a better idea if you imagine a cross between a milk wagon and an ice wagon. It is drawn by two native ponies. Each pair of ponies runs five or six miles, then it is changed. The ponies usually go at a gallop, and if the load is not too heavy and the road smooth they get over the ground pretty quickly. But country ponies have minds of their own. Sometimes they refuse to stir, at least forward. Backwards they will go any distance just for the pleasure of spilling both the "tika" and its occupant in the ditch.

When the ponies have once made up their minds, all the shouting and whipping and Hindustani abuse fail to move them an inch. The driver and conductor, or carriage-man, will both have to get down; calling all the people in the neighborhood to help them, they will have to push both the ponies and the carriage for some distance until the ponies get tired of the game and make a new start. Of course all this takes time, but in a country where the natives have a dozen million re-carnations to look forward to, time is of small object.

For all-around usefulness and, perhaps, also for speed, one will find that the bullock-cart is as good as anything invented. It is a two-wheeled cart with a cover to it; in appearance it is not unlike a small prairie schooner. The cover is made from bamboo matting and is open at both ends. Inside there is just room enough for a man to stretch out.

The cart is drawn by two patient hump-shouldered bullocks. On the pole in front of the cart and within easy reach of the bullocks' tails the driver is perched. The average speed is two miles an hour, but if the driver has a pair of good lungs and can shout continually and is persevering in twisting the animals' tails the speed may be accelerated by an additional half mile per hour.

If your cart is supplied with springs and the road is somewhat smooth, this way of traveling need not be entirely uncomfortable. At any rate you feel that you get a fair training in the virtue of patience. But when the cart is devoid of springs and the road is rough, you have rather a hard time of it, being slung from side to side and sometimes almost standing on your head. In vain you repeat the old couplet you learned at school:

> "Now patience is the pill
> That eases every ill."

BULLOCK CART.

You begin to imagine that some of your ribs are broken and that your hip-joints are dislocated, so you get out and walk on ahead for some distance and sit down by the roadside to wait for your "pullman car" to overtake you. Usually one travels by night in bullock-carts, because when one gets used to the shouting and bumping one can sleep and forget.

There is yet another quite common way of getting about the country, that is to be carried by coolies. Two long bamboo poles are tied one on each side of an ordinary dining-room chair. Seated in this chair four men will carry their passenger high in the air, placing the poles on their shoulders. There are also chairs called "dandies" made especially for the purpose of carrying people. Some of them can be quite comfortable. Then there is the "palke," or palanquin, a box-like affair with a pole sticking out at each end. This also is carried by four men.

At first it rather goes against the grain to be carried by your fellowmen. You do not like the idea at all. The only cure for that feeling is walking. You follow the men carrying the empty chair for a mile or two, perhaps under the hot Indian sun. Little by little you find your scruples vanishing. When the question is reduced to the alternative of dying from heat apoplexy far away from home and native land, or being carried by some coolies, who are used to that kind of work and even make a living by it, then it is wonderful how fast one's ideas change and adjust themselves to circumstances.

Once I had to go to the railway station twenty miles away. It was in the rainy season. My pony was dead. I had no alternative. It was either walk, or get people to carry me.

There was an old "dandy" in the veranda of our bungalow, an heirloom of some kind which a predecessor had left. We repaired it a little and thought it would be all right to use. I engaged eight carriers so that they might change off, and started before daylight. This was my first experience of being carried by men.

About seven miles from home, as we were going along at a good rate and I was enjoying the beautiful morning, crash went the dandy. I found myself on my seat of honor in the middle of the road with the bearers standing about gazing at me in open mouthed astonishment.

Over the remains of the "dandy" we held a short inquest, the verdict of which was that if we were to get to

CARRIED IN A DANDY.

the railway station at all it would not be in this conveyance. It was a total wreck. Like the famous "One Horse Shay," it went all to pieces and beyond repairs.

There was a Hindu village near by. We brought the wrecked dandy along as evidence and proceeded to the house of the village constable. He and his family came out and salaamed. We addressed him. He saw our plight. Would he lend us a little bedstead or a stool, or some contrivance, so that we might proceed on our journey?

O dear no! he was a poor man and had no beds. Both he and his children had to sleep on the floor. We should have to excuse him. We might ask the village headman,

THE PALKE.

perhaps he was able to help us, but as to him, he was so very poor!

The bearers, however, would not take no for an answer. They entered his yard and returned with a small bedstead just suitable for our purpose, and a pair of long poles. These things they held up before him while they gave expression of their opinions, both of the constable and his forefathers, for not being willing to help a Saheb when he was in need. This lecture and a little coin put into his palm limbered him up to such a degree that I am sure we could have taken all his beds and all his poles. Nothing he had was to good for us now.

We were soon under way again in our new conveyance. But I must tell you what a bedstead is. It is a wooden frame with a post or leg in each corner. Over this framework twine is stretched or woven in a clever way and the bed is ready. A mat or a blanket is all that is necessary to spread over the closely-woven bottom to make it quite comfortable.

A bed is called a "charpoi" in Hindustani. "Char" means four and "poi" means feet. A story is told of a Bengali babu who was in some sort of government service. On being transferred to another location he brought all his goods and chattels to the railway station to have them sent by train. Besides knowing a little English he had learned enough Latin to translate "charpoi" literally. So he put on the list of things to be sent, a "Quadruped." He was greatly astonished when the European station-master informed him that animals could not be sent by that train.

Of course, if one is rich he can keep an elephant. From ancient times elephants have been the steeds of royalty in India. If you are on friendly terms with a rajah in your neighborhood he will lend you an elephant now and then. Elephant-riding is all right if you do not take too much of it at a time.

Once while out in camp we went to visit a few Christian families living back among the hills, where there were no roads. We arranged to have an elephant take us back in the evening to our camp. It was a big, lumbering, good-natured animal. His master, the so-called "mahut," could make him perform several tricks. On a command from the "mahut the elephant ,would curl his trunk upward, touch his forehead and bow to you. That was his greeting or salaam. He would also throw his trunk back and open his mouth and let you examine his teeth. And a good solid set he had! Then he would let the mahut do some acro-

CLIMBING UP ON THE ELEPHANT.

batic performances on his long white tusks. Of course he was entitled to a few lumps of sugar after these performances.

When we were to mount, the mahut ordered the elephant to lie down. This he did by putting his forefeet forward and his hindlegs backwards, and sinking slowly to the ground. Then a great mattress, or pad, was placed on his back and tied with stout ropes. When everything was ready the mahut asked us to mount. This was more easily said than done. But the mahut rose to the occasion. Standing on one of the hind legs, which protruded like a log from under the great body, he caught the elephant's tail and held it so that it formed a loop. Then he told us to step on to

the other hindleg and from there by putting a foot into the loop and catching hold of the ropes, to climb up. By following these instructions and recieving a little assistance, my wife managed to get settled on the broad back of the elephant. After her, our daughter and I scrambled up in turn.

With the mahut in front and our whole family on his back, the elephant must have felt quite crowded. With a groan he began to move. First one end was raised, then the other. We clung to the ropes for dear life. That is the older members of the family did; the younger one clung to her father and shouted: "Let me down or I shall faint." But it was to late, the great body had begun to move. Confidence was soon restored and we had an enjoyable time.

Passing through the jungle the elephant would avoid all low branches — which, if he had passed under them, would have swept us off his back or, worse yet, left us suspended, like Absalom! but when he passed under a banyan tree he invariably broke off a branch or two to chew as he walked along.

Presently we came to a stream. Very carefully he climbed down the steep bank. In the middle of the stream he stopped to have a drink. He put his trunk into the water, sucked in a few gallons, opened his mouth and squirted the water down into his cavernous stomach. When he had satisfied the cravings of his inside he thought of his outside. A bath suggested itself to his mind and he at once started to take one. It was a shower bath. Had not the mahut protested in time we should all have been included in it, but, as it was, we got only a few stray drops. At sunset we arrived at the rest-house. There our animal laid down again and we slid to the ground.

SERVANTS.

One of the necessary evils a European in India has to put up with is servants. He needs them to look after his comforts. The great trouble is that he has to have such a number of them. At home one single girl will do nearly all the work of an entire household, while out here about a dozen men are required.

First you must have a cook. All over the world the cook is an important person, but in this land his importance is almost majestic. It would not do to address him as His Exellency; His Majesty would be more proper. And if he gives you good things to eat you will have no objection to addressing him in any term that will suit him, or his position.

The jungle missionary lives in a straw-thatched bungalow, behind which are a few small houses. One of these is the kitchen. There the cook reigns supreme. You will look in vain for a cook stove or range. All you will find is an open fireplace and a few pots and pans. However, that does not hinder him in the exploitation of his art. He will send up to your table a dish that tastes and looks like beef steak, and yet you know all the time that you are eating chicken. Beef is to be had only in the large cities. Yes, and what is more, he can with a little anchovy sauce and some tricks of his trade cause the white meat of a chicken to appear like fish.

SERVANTS.

There is almost no end to his inventions. Especially in connection with chicken, he is a perfect juggler. Small wonder that he is so important! The welfare of the whole family is in his hands.

The cook has to have an assistant. He is called "pani-walla," or water carrier. With a bamboo pole, from which are suspended a pair of earthenware vessels or a pair of empty kerosene tins, across his shoulders, he goes to the spring or well or pond as the case may be for the daily supply of water. Then he has to make the fire, chop wood,

THE PANIWALLA.

scour pots and pans, in short, do most of the work of the cook at whose beck and call he must always be. There is more work than dignity connected with his position.

Next, there is the bearer, or house servant. This man has to keep the house in order and wait on the table. Usually his work does not keep him long. He finds lots of time to hang about the kitchen or to try to work the tickle out of his tongue with his particular crony in the shade of some mango tree in the compound. Yet if you call him he is at your elbow almost in an instant, ready to do your bidding.

Next to claim your attention is the Dhoby. You must have heard of the Dhoby. He is the famous washerman of India. On Monday morning he calls for the wash and Saturday evening he brings it back clean, crisp, starched and ironed. He brings it in a big bundle on his back, except when it is very heavy; then his wife brings the bundle on her head. It isn't the style here for men to carry anything on their heads.

The washerman takes your clothes to the pond, and by a dexterous set of manipulations perfected by generation after generation of Dhobies, dips the dirty garment into the dirty water and beats it against a dirty stone with the result that he can deliver it to you clean. It is quite a sight to see a number of Dhobies at work about a pond beating clothes against stones. When Mark Twain first saw them he thought they were trying to crack the stones with wet clothes.

The Dhoby neither gives nor implies any guarantee not to tear your garments or to pound any buttons to pieces. The owner has to take all those risks.

If you have a horse it is also necessary for you to keep a servant called a "syce." The name is Hindustani and several "sizes" too small for the position. His work is to look after the horse, clean it, feed it, and saddle it when the master calls for it.

If he is a member of the Hindu caste whose caste-work it is to take care of horses, the "syce" will want a helper to do the work for him. It would be below him to go out and cut an armful of grass for the horse. He must have a man of a lower caste to do the work. In the meantime the "syce" will sit on his heels and smoke his "huka" and draw his pay.

Often it is not possible for a missionary to get a proper supply of milk from the village, he must keep his own

VILLAGE WASHER-MAN OR DHOBY.

cows. If he has cows he must also have a cowman to take care of them. The cowman's duties are to feed the cows, herd them, bring them to the back door of the bungalow morning and evening and milk them.

In America, milking a cow is not regarded as a very difficult operation. Nearly everybody in the country districts knows how to milk. Out here in Santalistan it is quite different. You need only to watch the cowman once to find that out. First the milch-cow is brought and tied to a post, and a pail of feed is put before her. Then to prevent her kicking, the cowman ties both her hind legs together— that is if she is a kicker. These preliminaries ready, the calf is brought. No cow will give her milk without having her calf with her. When the calf has sucked a while the cowman's assistant drags it away, and the cowman proceeds to extract the balance of the milk, often under the most violent protest from the cow. To make up a single quart of milk several cows are often called upon to contribute. The small Santal cow is a better fighter than milker.

If the calf dies the cow will not let herself be milked. The cowman will then try a ruse. He will stuff the skin of the dead calf, mount it on legs and bring it out at milkingtime for the poor mother to look and smell at. The ruse is often successful and the sight of the stuffed calf will make the cow give her milk.

We have named only the most important servants as we find them in the humble bungalow of the jungle missionary. In large and wealthy households there is simply no limit to the number of servants employed.

But why keep so many?

Again we run up against the influence of the caste system. A man born a sweeper must remain a sweeper. A man born a cook must remain a cook. It is the work of his caste. No one else will do his work, neither will he do the work of others. In short, this is a land of specialists.

Apart from this reason more people are really required to attend to the work of a household in this country because everything is so unhandy. Water often has to be brought from a long ways off. Grass for the horses and cows the same. Owing to the hot climate many of the supplies can only be kept in small quantities. For the same reason food cannot very well be kept over from one day to the next, something which involves both extra work and waste.

MILKING A COW.

To take care of a house properly also means a great deal more work than at home. The white ants are very destructive. They work while you sleep. Every corner of the house must be watched daily for signs of their activity. Every hole and crevice becomes the hidingplace of reptiles and insects. Hosts of creeping, flying, jumping things will take up their abode with you if you are not on the alert.

In a well ordained household the servants are required

to wear a sort of livery or uniform. If this rule were not enforced, they would perhaps in the hot weather appear with nothing on but a strip of loincloth. The house servants usually wear a long white coat, or rather a combination between a coat and a nightshirt. On their heads they wear a turban called a puggree. To wind a turban properly is quite an art. They take a piece of thin muslin cloth some fifteen yards long and wind it about their heads in any shape they might fancy. There are as many shapes and fashions of servant's turbans out here as there are shapes and fashions of women's headgear at home.

The outdoor servants wear jackets, the style, shape and color of which is usually left to their own fancy.

But this reminds me—.

Some time ago I paid a short visit to a neighbor missionary. It was in the beginning of the cold season and the evenings were delightful. We sat out on the steps in front of the bungalow and watched the stars being lit. We talked about home and our dear ones far across the seas and exchanged experiences in our work. After a while conversation drifted on to other subjects and we fell to talking about servants.

The missionary's wife told the following story: "Some years ago high sleeves were the fashion in women's dresses. Last time we were home on furlough, I brought with me several waists of that style. They were too heavy and warm for this country and I did not use them much so they got motheaten. One day in the rainy season I looked them over and found that they were eaten beyond repair, so I threw them away.

During the following cold season we went to Calcutta to meet some friends and bring them out to our station for a short visit. We ordered our syce to bring the horse and carriage to the railway station on a certain day when we would arrive with our guests. Imagine my mortification when on alighting from the train our syce comes up to us salaaming very politely, arrayed in one of my castaway motheaten, highsleeved waists!

Every European in India will have to learn, sometimes

THE VILLAGE BARBER.

through costly experience, that all servants are not quite honest, at least not so honest as they profess to be. The first servant we engaged was a Madrassy, that is, a man from the Madras presidency. We engaged him on the recommendation of older missionaries and because he could talk a little English. He had to have one month's wages in advance. Well, after being with us four or five days he dissapeared into the mystic Indian night and we have never seen him since.

You have to learn by experience how to deal with servants. When you are a stranger they usually take you in.

ON THE WAY TO THE WELL.

THE MISSIONARY AS A DOCTOR.

A missionary out in the jungle, far away from doctors and hospitals will by necessity be driven to "practice medicine," no matter whether he likes to or not. People find their way to him with their complaints. He is their father and mother, he must help them. As to his ability to help they have no doubt, for is he not a Saheb? And Sahebs know everything.

When people have become Christians they have, of course no more faith in their old medicinemen and cannot employ them. Their medicines are given in connection with offerings to the "Bongas," or evil spirits, and that practice of course, is out of the question for Christians. Therefore when there is sickness in the Christian native family they naturally turn to the missionary. He must help them. And so it happens that the missionary and his wife must "rush in where angels fear to tread." They must begin to "practice."

First you send for some manual of medicine.

People tell you that homeopathic medicines are the best for you to use. They are cheap and easy to take. Only three drops in a little water, and you do not run any risk of overdosing your patients. If it does not cure it certainly doesn't kill, and that a great consolation, because directions are not always followed out as carefully as they should be.

Two men once came to the missionary to consult him about their grandmother's uncle's sister-in-law, or whatever the relation was, that is only a matter of minor detail. Well, they explained their relation's symptoms and answered all questions the missionary put to them. They had brought a bottle, a thing patients often fail to do, — expecting the Saheb to furnish them with one. There was a crack however in the bottle, they had brought; but on their assuring him that it did not leak he thought it would do. He then filled it half full of water, counted into it 27 drops of homeopathic fluid, and told them to give the patient an oystershell full three times a day for three days and after that to return for more. They made salaams and were off.

On the way home through some accident the crack opened so that the bottle began to leak. They sat down by the roadside and held a consultation. What was to be done? The precious medicine was slowly dripping away without doing anyone a bit of good. The medicine would be wasted and they would have their long walk for nothing. Rather than lose it they decided then and there to drink it themselves. So each drank half of the contents of the bottle and was none the worse for it.

One objection to the giving of homeopathic medicine to ablebodied Santals is that it tastes very little different from water. In fact it is hard for them to believe that it is medicine at all. For such cases one must give Pain Killer or some similar strong decoction. One takes a spoonful of

THE OLD MISSION HOUSE, KAERABANI.

this, mixes a little quinine into it, and gives it to the patient in a little cold water. The patient will shed a few tears, the taste will abide with him all day, but he will never for a moment doubt that it was a dose of real medicine he took. Often after such a dose the patient will clear his throat, wipe his eyes and say, "This ought to cure me.".

But I must tell you about Puchia. He and his family had been Christians for about a year and during that time every thing had gone well with them. But one day he sent word to the mission that he was very sick and asked us to send him some medicine. As we did not know what was ailing him we sent one of the preachers over to diagnose the case. He found that Puchia was suffering from fever, a cold, and an attack of colic. Medicine was prepared to meet all these symptoms. Directions were given that the Pain Killer should be taken at once to relieve his stomach, in a couple of hours he should take a fever-reducing draught and when the hot stage was passed he should take a dose of quinine. This last was to be repeated daily for three days.

After taking the Pain Killer Puchia felt better, so much so that he was able to begin to reason with himself, that, if one dose of the medicine helped him so much, it was only reasonable to expect that if he took them all at once he would get well all the sooner.

He then asked his wife to fetch him all the medicines. Although she protested, he drank all the aconite in the bottle, ate all the quinine we had put up for him, and then turned over on his mat and went to sleep. This was in the morning. All that day and the following night he slept. The next day towards noon he awoke completely cured. He never tired of extolling the power of the missionary's medicine.

One soon becomes familiar with certain common recurrent complaints and their remedies. There is a skin disease, or itch, very common in the cold season, when people do not bathe as often as they should. One finds that it yields to treatment with sulphur, and people are very thankful to get rid of it.

About four and a half million people die every year in India from malaria. For this there is one principal remedy quinine. And it is easy to administer, as the Government prepares it and sells it at all the postoffices throughout the land. It is put up in little envelopes containing one dose, and each costing half a cent. But quinine is bitter and very few people think it palatable, therefore one must see that one's patients take it. It is always safest to have them take it in your presence.

Sometimes people bring their blind to the missionary asking him to restore their eyesight, or their deaf ones, with the request that their hearing might be restored. When they come thus one always gets a chance to speak to them about the Great Healer who has come to heal all their diseases.

There is no end to the variety of cases brought in. There are boils to be opened, sores to be cleansed and bandaged, and broken bones to be set. One must do his best to help relieve their sufferings. After awhile the Mem Saheb will specialize on women's and children's diseases, and the Saheb on the men's ills and the surgical cases.

One day a man living eight miles from the mission station having heard of the wonderful power of the missionaries brought his case to the Mem Saheb. The difficulty was this: A few days previously his buffalo cow had calved. And though it was her own offspring, she was so perverse and so unnatural a mother that she refused to suckle it. Could the Mem Saheb give him some medicine that would make the cow suckle her calf?

The Mem Stheb was sorry she had no cattle medicine. The man had to return with an empty bottle.

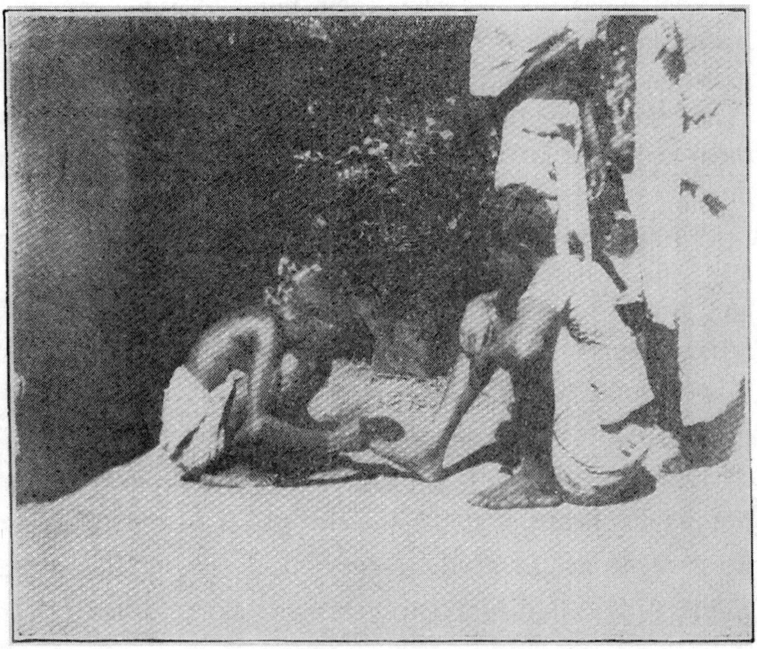

BARBER PARING TOE-NAILS.

THE MISSIONARY AS A PEACE-MAKER.

A missionary among a childish people like the Santals soon learns that his work is not finished when he has preached his sermon on Sunday. He must not only be their religious teacher but their guide to better things in every field. His relation to his flock will be like that of a father to his children. If they are sick they come to the missionary, if they are in want he is their refuge. So also when they quarrel, to the missionary they come with their complaints.

Early this morning the whole adult male population from one of the nearest villages arrived and asked to have a little talk with the Padre. The headman came forward and said:

"For two days we have tried to settle a dispute between Lalu and Karan, but without success, now we have brought them here to ask you if you will be kind enough to help us."

Karan and Lalu came forward and on being asked what the trouble was between them, they both started to talk at once and evidently laboring under the illusion that the Padre was deaf. During a little lull in their vociferous expostulations the Padre got a chance to ask:

"Who told you I was deaf?"

"No one has told us that," was the reply.

"Now don't you try to fool me," the Padre continued. "someone must have tried to slander me and told you that I was almost stone deaf and that you had to shout at the top of your voices to make me hear. Do tell me the name of the rascal and I shall make him limp. — I can hear as well as any of you."

These or similar remarks usually break the spell, the excitement subsides and one can get down to business.

In this case it appeared that Karan had lent Lalu 30 cents a year and a half ago. For this sum Karan was to have the privilege of using one of Lalu's fields for three years. The headman and several neighbors were witnesses to the transaction. Karan had worked the field one year and was beginning to prepare it for the second year's planting when Lalu went to the field and forbid him to touch it. Lalu wanted to work his own field after this. Hot words fell on both sides but, fortunately, they did not come to blows.

In the Santal Parganas this transaction is illegal. A Santal has no right to sell the use of his fields in this way, and if such cases are brought into the courts both parties are liable to be punished.

Lalu was asked why he had backed out of his part of the contract. He replied that he thought Karan had got much more than the amount he lent him from the one crop he had reaped.

Karan was then asked to show how much paddy he had raised on the field last year. He gave the amount, and when the cost of working the field was deducted a net profit of 25 cents was left. This left a balance of five cents of the loan besides interest for a year and a half.

"For what purpose did you borrow the money, Lalu?"

"My cows were put in the pound and I had to pay damages to get them out," was the reply.

"Karan helped you when you was in trouble. You give him your word of honor as a man that he could have the use of this field for three years, but after he had used it only one year you not only break your promise but drive him from the field. This is not a man's act but that of a child. You promise to pay Karan the balance of the debt next fall, but, will he believe you? You have proved before all of us how much your word is to be depended on. You have broken your word once, you are able to do so again. Apart from the fact that your transaction is illegal, three years is too long a time. Two years would have been ample. Karan ought not to have taken advantage of his neighbor when he was in need. Christ has told us that we should love one another and help each other in time of need.

Lalu was asked to pay the balance of his debt in the presence of the assembly. He managed to raise the required sum, paid it over, peace was restored and the two men promised never to quarrel again.

Domestic quarrels are not uncommon and calls for both delicate and diplomatic treatment.

A few evenings ago a woman came to tell the Padre that she was not going to live with her husband any more She said:

"I will not stay with that brute any longer. You have married me to him and now you must release me. I shall never darken that man's door again. The world is big, I can go anywhere, but back to him, never, never!"

"What has happened?"

"My husband abused me, called me a witch and at last he gave me a beating. Look at my shoulder here and my arms and see for yourself.—I'll never go back to him!"

There were bruises on her arms and one of her shouders, which bore testimony to the fact, that if they were inflicted by her husband, he had certainly not spared the rod.

The woman was asked to spend the night with her brother who lived in the nearest village. In the morning her case would be looked into. Her husband would be called and everything done to straighten matters out.

"But, my baby! Why doesn't my husband bring the baby?"

"Let the baby stay with its father tonight, it will be quite all right. You stay with your brother tonight and come over tomorrow morning."

At dawn the next morning the woman was at the mission. Restlessly she walked up and down the road waiting for her husband to appear. After a night away from her baby and her home, things began to look different. When the husband arrived, it was but the work of a few minutes to get each one to admit his share of the blame and to ask forgiveness. Then both knelt at the throne of grace and asked their heavenly Father to forgive them.

They admitted that they had been careless of late. Their family altar had been neglected and they had become very slack in church going. The enemy had seen his chance to get in between them.

They said goodbye and started for home. The husband walked ahead and the wife with her child astride her hip followed five or six paces behind, but everybody who saw them knew that they went home to live their second honeymoon.

SALKU AND HIS PIG.

A Santal village is quite democratic in its government, There is a set of officers generally elected by the villagers themselves. The leader is the village chief or headman, called "Manjhi." He has an assistant called "Paranik." There is also a village messenger and a priest or two. Beside these there is yet another important officer, the "Jog-Manjhi" whose duties are many and difficult to describe; suffice it to say that he is more or less responsible for the morals of the young people in the village.

Any villager can bring his or her troubles to the headman, who must hear them patiently and if he finds the case of sufficient importance he will send the messenger to call the villagers together and they will sit on the case. Every adult residing in the village has not only a right to a seat in the village council but has a right to partake in its deliberations.

After hearing a case the village assembly will pass judgement, and although the case may subsequently be brought into the law-courts the judge or magistrate will as a rule uphold the decision of the village assembly.

According to western ideas of justice, many of the decisions of the village council are queer, but as long as they themselves are satisfied and their troubles are settled peaceably, why should outsiders complain? Naturally it is only petty cases they can decide, such as small property cases, social questions, and matters pertaining to witches. Litigation of this kind they enjoy. The villagers will leave

BRINGING THE PIG HOME.

their work and sit for a whole day discussing from every possible and impossible standpoint a case involving the value of a few pennies.

But I must tell you about Salku and his pig.

Salku is a heathen living in one of the nearest villages. Many of his neighbors and relatives have become Christians, but he has always hidden behind some excuse. However, he is very friendly and often comes to the mission.

One day both Salku and his wife came to us in great excitement. They complained that Sitol, a Christian neighbor of theirs, had killed their pig. It was the only pig they had, and they were very much attached to it and felt the loss keenly. Would not the missionary, who is their father and mother, compel Sitol to give them another pig, a live one in place of the one he had killed?

Now it is Santal law that if a pig strays into a man's field and does damage, the owner of the field is at liberty to kill the pig and keep the head and one forepart for himself; the rest of the animal he must make over to the owner. Among neighbors in the same village, however, it is the custom to warn a man two or three times, and, if he still persists in letting his pig run at large, it will subsequently be killed.

This was in the spring, and Sitol had just planted his corn. Salku's pig, who had in some way found this out, went to Sitol's field, started to root out the corn and eat it. Sitol was not at all pleased wih this performance. He drove the pig away and sent word to its owner to take care of it. But Sitol had no sooner returned to his house than the pig was there again plowing crooked furrows across his cornfield.

Sitol lost his temper, got his bow and arrows, went to the field and the result was that Salku lost his pig. Having cut away his rightful share Sitol called Salku to take away what was left. But this he refused to do.

He said to Sitol: "What am I to do with a dead pig? Give me a live one as good as the one you have killed, otherwise I will go to the Saheb and complain."

Of course, there was no settlement. Sitol's temper was

up and there were hot words on both sides, so they left the dead pig on the field and Salku and his wife came to the mission.

After asking them a few questions as to how it all came about, I told them that the best thing they could do was to go home, take charge of their parts of the animal and say

REMOVING THE BRISTLES.

nothing more about it. Afterwards I would investigate the case, and if Sitol was at fault we would compel him to make good the loss.

But Salku persisted that he would not touch the dead pig. What he wanted was a live one. I tried to tell him that a pig, like a miser, was no good to anybody until it was dead. But all my arguments were in vain. Salku knew what he wanted, and that was a live pig.

"Well," I said, "you must go to the village headman and complain. When the villagers gather to hear your case I will send some of my men over to help you and see that justice is done."

The same afternoon the villagers were called together and the trial began. In the examination it appeared that Sitol had warned his neighbor only once that his pig was doing damage. That was wrong of him. He should at least have warned him twice. Therefore he was guilty of wrong-doing. To this everybody agreed.

Sitol was found guilty.

The next question to be settled was this: What right had Salku to let his pig run at large at this time of the year, when people were putting in their crops? Everyone else in the village had his pigs tied or herded. All agreed that Salku had absolutely no right to let his pig run about at its own pleasure.

Salku was also found guilty.

The next question to be solved was whether they were both equally guilty, or if one offence was greater than the other.

One of the village patriarchs spoke up and said: "I think they are both equally guilty. They have both done wrong and should be punished equally."

This opinion was received with a general murmur of assent. The headman then asked in what the punishment should consist, but, as no one ventured to propose anything he asked three of the village fathers to go aside and agree on a motion to lay before the assembly. After a short deliberation they returned with this proposal that each of the two litigants should pay a fine of one rupee, four annas, a sum which equals about forty cents in American money.

Such fines when realized are as a rule divided equally among the villagers who took part in the case. They either divide the money, or buy a goat or a pig for it and divide the meat, or—which is the most common among the

FEASTING.

heathen—they go to the nearest drink shop and buy rice-beer for it. But according to Santal ideas it is neccessary that such fines be spent in eating or drinking, so that the offence may be removed. The sin of the offender is "eaten" by those who judged him. Afterwards no one has a right to throw the offence into his face again, his sin has been eaten and digested, as they express it. Should any one bring up the offence again he makes himself liable to punishment by his fellow villagers.

But there was yet another riddle to be solved before the days work was done. What was to be done with the dead pig?

After long and profound deliberations it was finally agreed that Sitol should return the part he had taken away and that the whole pig should be divided into two equal parts. One part should be given to Sitol and the other to Salku. Both men had been equally guilty of wrong-doing, both had been fined equally, therefore it was only just that both should share equally in the pig. The fact of the original ownership of the pig was entirely lost in the deep deliberations of the assembly.

Sitol took the part decreed to him, sold enough of the meat to pay his fine and had a feast with his family on the remainder. For them it was a joyous event, as the times were hard and it was not often that they could afford to have meat. Salku, the original owner of the pig, did the same with his share but unfortunately his residue after having sold enough to pay his fine was a very small one. However, both parties were perfectly satisfied with the outcome of the case. They went home as good friends as ever. Their troubles had been adjusted by the village council.

THE SACRED BULL.

Beldangal is a large Hindu village. There are ruins in it of old Hindu temples and palaces, but the glories of the place all lie in the past, the hazy, dreamy past of Hindustan. The present picture shows a couple of rows of low, straw-thatched, illkept mud-houses, a crooked, dirty street with a few goats, calves and naked children.

Many of the villagers are Brahmins. They are holy men and priests of Siva, Ram, Krishna and the millions of other gods of Hinduism. In fact, the Brahmin himself is a god and is worshipped as such. All Hindus of the lower castes must bow down before the Brahmin and worship him. If a Brahmin comes to the house of a low-caste man he must be entertained with the best the house can afford. But first of all his feet must be washed in a bowl and the host drink a a mouthful of that dirty water. By drinking that water the man acquires merit and believes that his sins are washed away.

Some years ago there lived an old Brahmin in this village. He was quite rich, but he was old and feeble and felt that the end was drawing near. Like a wise man he began to prepare himself so that he could meet death in the right way.

The first thing he did was to look about for a suitable bull calf, whose tail he could clasp in his dying hand and into which his soul could pass when it should have to leave the body. He was anxious about his next incarnation.

HINDU WORSHIPPER.

What if he should be sent to earth again to occupy the body of a snake, a dog or a sow? The very thought filled him with horrors. He must find a bull calf.

In a Santal village close by, a suitable calf was at last found. After due bickering it was purchased and brought to the Brahmin's house and tied close at hand should it be suddenly needed.

In due course the Brahmin died clasping the calf's tail. As soon as his struggles were over, the preparations for his cremation were begun. The priests gathered. Holy water from the Ganges was sprinkled on the bull calf and he was consecrated to Siva. Then they branded it on both hindquarters, on one side with the image of the lotus flower and on the other with the trident, or the three-tined fork of Siva.

The Brahmin's body, the bull calf and a number of things necessary to the various ceremonies were then brought out to a large pond near the village where the funeral pyre had already been built.

With due ceremonies the body was put on the pyre. The eldest son applied the torch to the wood with his own hand, and all that was mortal of the old Brahmin was reduced to ashes. While this was going on, the calf was brought forward and the eldest son, in the name of his departed father, grasped it by the tail, drove it out into the pond and forced it to swim across. When the other bank was reached the boy let go of the tail and the ceremony, so far as the calf was concerned, was over.

The calf was now a sacred bull. No one was allowed to tie him or use him for any work, and he was free to wander about wherever he pleased.

No sooner had the calf found out that he was free than it started for its native village. Nearly all the people there are Santals and have no great respect for sacred bulls. From door to door it was beaten and abused, and for a while it had a daily struggle to obtain food.

But as the days passed by he grew to be a large and strong bull and soon found that he no longer needed to run away from the little shepherd boys, but rather that they would flee before his horns. He tried larger boys and the experiment usually came out the same way, they fled. At last he tried grown-up men, and his experience was that in most cases his warlike appearence, flourishing horns, pawing and bellowing would put even them to rout. The Santals whispered to one another that a Hindu "Bonga" had taken possession of the bull, and they gave him a wide berth.

In this way the sacred bull became a first class nuisance in the village. If a woman spread her grain on the ground to dry, the bull would be there to eat it. All her shouting and flourishing of stick availed nothing.

In the first part of June every year the farmers sow their paddy, or rice, in hotbeds so as to get the plants ready to set out as soon as the rains come. At this time of the year these hotbeds are the only green patches on the landscape. No wonder these patches were a source of temptation to the sacred bull!

Before dawn one morning an old Santal found the bull in the middle of his hotbed munching the young, green shoots. This was going a little too far, the old man thought. His temper was up. Back to the house he went to fetch an ax and a rope.

In a short time the spirit of the Brahmin was again homeless, and all the Santals in the village knew before sunrise that under a certain matkom tree at the edge of the woods there was fresh beef to be had.

The entire Santal population of the village feasted. And it was the understanding that no tongue should wag about that matter, but that everybody should go home and forget where the beef came from. And had the old man not been indiscreet, the story would perhaps have ended here, but his avarice led him into trouble.

He cured the hide of the sacred bull and took it to market. The hide merchant, on examining it noticed the brands.

Crowds of Hindus soon gathered around and some one recognized the hide as the one which once covered the sacred bull of Beldangal.

The Hindus were in a rage and threatened the old man with violence. "Think of it," they said, "the Santals have killed a sacred bull and perhaps even eaten it!"

SIRDARS.

The old man was then taken to the Sirdar, who is a sort of head of the village watchmen in the district. The Sirdar was a Santal living in the same village as the offender, and had likely eaten his share of the beef. However, in his official capacity he called the villagers together and made out a list of some twenty families who had partaken of the feast. The people were thoroughly frightened and wondered what punishment would be meted out to them. The Sirdar held the opinion that they would all have to go to jail; still if each family would give him two rupees, he said, he would square matters with the Hindus and the whole thing would soon blow over.

Some days passed and the Brahmins in Beldangal became impatient. The Santals had not been punished as they thought they ought to be, so the Brahmins went and called in another Sirdar, a Hindu. This new referee investigated the case, first in the village of the Santals; then he took seven or eight of the leaders with him to his own village six miles away, where he kept them for two days and, according to the custom of his ilk, tried to squeeze heavy bribes from them.

But the Santals finally grew tired of this procedure and agreed among themselves that it was best for them to go directly to the magistrate, confess everything, and take their punishment at his hands like men.

The magistrate called in the two Sirdars and the Santals and held a searching inquiry, under which the work of those two men came out in a rather unfavorable light. The Santal Sirdar having returned the rupees, he had taken and being shielded by his people escaped punishment, but the Hindu Sirdar was fined heavily, and barely escaped losing his post for the part he had played.

The magistrate then asked the Santals which of them had killed the bull?

An old wrinkled Santal came forward, bowed low, and said: "Your Honor, I killed it."

The magistrate laughed and said: "Is is possible that an old man like you singlehanded could kill a large strong bull?" But all the villagers declared that what he said was true. The magistrate then put his hand into his pocket, brought out two rupees, gave them to the old man, and told him to go home.

Through this experience both Hindus and Santals have found out that before the law there is no difference between a sacred bull and a common plow bullock, and that, as the sacred bull had no home and no owner responsible for it, in the event it becomes a public nuisance, it as a good riddance to kill it.

The Brahmins complain that since the Englishmen became the rulers of this country justice is not to be had. The most awful crimes, even the killing of sacred bulls, remain unpunished.

On the other hand the Santals never tire of singing the praises of the English magistrate. They say: "The Salieb does not look at the face of the Brahmin, neither does he look at the face of the Santal, but he deals out justice equally to all."

SANTAL CHRISTIANS.

RELIGIOUS QUARRELS

In many of the villages in Santalistan the population is a very mixed one. A dozen or more Hindu castes may be represented, each with its own gods, worship and ceremonies. But that does not matter so long as the people are all Hindus. The power of the Brahmin holds them together.

With Mohammedans it is different. They have very little in common with the Hindus, and it is not infrequent that Hindus and Moslems step on each others' religious corns.

A short way from the Mission station there is a large village. The most of its inhabitants are Hindus of the various castes but there are also a number of Mohammedan families.

Some time ago a babajee, or religious mendicant, came to the village, ostensibly to strengthen the faith of the Hindus. He was quite modern in his methods. Among other things he carried with him an accordion, a patched and scarred veteran of many a compaign yet under the babajees trained hand an instrument capable of producing a series of the most wonderful sounds and noices ever invented by man.

The young men of the village were recruited to help. Some were put to beating drums, some to playing various stringed instruments, and some to dancing—all this to please and honor the gods and to procure an easy living for the babajee.

The Hindu villagers were highly delighted with the music, and enthusiasm grew fast. Every night the crowds would be larger, the music louder, and the shouting of the dancers more rapturous. All night long pandemonium reigned in the street.

After listening to this racket for a week or two the Mohammedans, of course, thought it was getting stale, and they began to protest against having their night's rest broken; but no one heeded them. At last they thought they could bear it no longer, therefore they raised a purse and bought an old cow. They bided their time till the crowds had gathered in the evening to resume their noisy dance. Then they butchered the cow in sight of the dancing Hindus just to see what would happen.

According to Hindu ideas to kill a cow, the most sacred animal, is considered one of the greatest crimes a human being can commit.

The killing of the cow stopped both the music and the dancing and so far proved effective, but as to restoring peace the measure was a total failure. It was rather like the upsetting of a beehive. The babajee preached a crusade against the Moslems and any longbearded follower of the illustrious prophet who dared show his head outside his door would at once be made a target for all sorts of missiles.

Fortunately most of the fighting in this country is done by windpower. It is a question of good strong lungs.

The Hindus would tell the Mohammedans what they thought of them, their fathers and forefathers for twenty generations back. And when the male line was finished opinion would be passed on their female line of forbears.

But the Mohammedans were not entirely without training in this sort of warfare. They thought of several spicy things to say about the Hindus, both of the present and the past generations, so the scores were about even.

When the Hindus saw that no satisfactory results were to be gained by verbal warfare they gathered a council of war to discuss the situation. In this they decided on a more modern way of silencing their antagonists. They declared a boycott. No Mussulman was to be allowed to draw water from the village ponds, and no Hindu was to buy from or sell anything to a Moslem, or to have any dealings with him of any nature whatever under penalty of being outcasted.

As to water, the boycott was of no inconvenience. It was just at the end of the rainy season and water was plentyful everywhere. But many of the Mahammedans were weavers and cloth merchants; and, when they found that they could obtain no space in the marketplace to exhibit their wares, they found the boycott not only an inconvenience but a serious loss to them, as it cut them off from their means of livelihood.

Several of the Moslem fathers then got together to consider what was to be done. After due smoking of "huka" and much stroking of beard it was decided that five of the most representative members of their clan should go to the magistrate of the district and lodge a complaint of unfair treatment against the owner of the marketplace.

"But," said one, "would it not be a good thing if we

could get the Padre to give us a letter to the magistrate? He knows all about our troubles and a few words from him would surely limber up the arm of the law and help us to secure speedy justice."

In consequence of his, three of the most longbearded and venerable fathers kissed the Moslem blarneystone—if such a thing exists—and came to the Mission. They found the Padre on the veranda and after deep salaams addressed him as follows: "We know that you are the father and mother of us all. Your blessings preserve our poor lives and there is no one like you in the land, and above you there is only one—Allah. Your Illustrious Presence knows that those worshippers of idols, our neighbors, are persecuting us and have forbidden us to sit in the market-place and sell our wares. Our children have become like shadows from hunger, and we ourselves are, as Your Higness well can see, bent with sorrow. In our trouble we have come to Your Highness with a little prayer. Would Your Highness make us and our children happy forever by giving us a little letter to the magistrate so that we might get speedy justice and these worshippers of idols be put to shame?"

"O yes, the Padre would gladly do that if he wanted your suit to be dismissed. But that he does not want. Look here, those magistrates are very suspicious people, that you know. Well, if you come to the magistrate with a letter from the Padre Saheb he will think, "Those men must have very little ground to stand on, as they have found it necessary to get support from a Padre.' And he will dismiss your case."

With more blarney about the wisdom of the Saheb they salaamed and went their way. The complaint was lodged with the magistrate of the district. He sent out two native deputy police inspectors to investigate the case on the spot. One of them was a Hindu and the other a Mohammedan.

Each inspector went to his own people and raised as much money among them as he could. Then the inspectors called both parties together for a heart to heart talk, in which they admonished them to make friends again and forget their quarrels. If not, they would have to take the leaders on both sides with them to jail, for they had both been found guilty of breach of the peace.

This threat was effectual. The complaint was withdrawn and peace settled again in the market-place under the mango trees.

VILLAGE CHARCOAL PEDLER.

MOSQUITOES AND OTHER INSECTS.

For a collector of bugs and insects Santalistan must be a veritable Eldorado with an inexhaustable supply of material. During the rainy season, especially, you will find insects and bugs everywhere, all kinds of them, describable ones as well as indescribable ones. If you light your lamp in the evening and forget to shut the doors or windows your table will soon be covered with the most wonderful collection of creeping, flying, jumping beings, many of them regular stinkpots. If you go out for a morning walk you will se big beetles rolling balls of cowdung along the road in front of you. Why they do it and where they are rolling them to only a bugologist can tell.

Then there are the armies of ants, always busy. Some dwell in trees, some in the ground. In well ordered regiments they move from one camp to another and you never get tired of watching them. If you turn over a leaf or a twig there are the white ants, a brotherhood,the members of which are past masters in the art of destruction. The white ant, they say, can eat and digest everything except, perhaps, tempered steel.

Someone has claimed that the Himalaya mountains once extended over half of India, but through the ages the white ants have eaten and digested the greater part of them, and they are still at the work. However we need have no fear that the great peaks will be destroyed during our lifetime as it is too cold for them up there to make fast progress.

THE WATERPOT SELLER.

White ants cannot endure the cold. So far they have limited their operations to the warm countries. Hot and sultry weather seems to stimulate them to extra activity. Their disposition is decidedly pessimistic. They always approach a thing from the dark side. They cannot stand the light.

In the morning you may discover a pile of wet dirt in

the corner of your room. Poke a stick into it and you will find it swarming with white ants. Unless your floor is made from good cement you had better not put your shoes there over night. If you do, you may find only the iron heel pegs left to wear the next morning.

One of our missionaries, while out on a preaching tour, once spent a night in a village temple. Thoughtlessly he put a certain garment of his on the floor beside his bed, and the result was that he had to wear his pajamas the next day.

On a hot sultry night a lady missionary took a mat and placed it on the ground in front of her bungalow, where she could get a little breeze. She fell soundly asleep. Toward morning she awoke with a cold creepy sensation about head. It did not take her long to find out that her hair was literally full of white ants, and she had to get busy to save herself from being scalped or at least made baldheaded.

The evil fame of the Indian mosquito has reached to the ends of the earth. Compared to him his American cousin is an aristocrat and a gentleman. He is a man of principle and full of business. He will come prospecting around your face, neck or hands, and when he finds a hopeful looking locality he at once gets out his drill and starts business. And if he has "struck oil" he will let himself be distracted by nothing, he will chose death rather than to be deprived of his business.

Not so the Indian mosquito. He will come to you under the guise of a philanthropist. He knows that your soul is starving for want of music, so he comes to sing to you. And he has a voice like a Scotch bagpipe. While he sings he will scout around for a favorable place to attack you. When his plans of attack are matured, he will call his caste-fellows and put some of them at diverting your at-

SANTAL SAW MILL.

tention, while he relieves you of some of your superfluous blood.

Now, if it were only the loss of a few gallons of blood, you might, perhaps, in time be able to forgive him his thieving propensities; but there are worse things to be said against him. He is a murderer. He will not kill you himself, oh no, he must not spoil his reputation as a philanthropist. His wife has to do that.

The females in one branch of the mosquito family, called the Anopheles, have been delegated to poison you. This they do by pumping into your blood the germs of Malaria. If enough of the germs have been injected into your veins, you get the dreadful fever.

You soon understand that the mosquito is your enemy, and you must get him, or he will ultimately get you. There can be no peace between you and him. You wage war against him in various ways. First by draining off all pools of stagnant water, or, if that is not possible, by pouring kerosene on them, for in such places the mosquitoes breed and multiply.

It is no easy matter to get the Santals to understand, that there is a connection between the pool of stagnant water and the man dying from malaria. You must demonstrate it to them. You take some stagnant water, in which there are a great number of those little wrigglers, or mosquito spawn, and put it in a bottle. Then you tie paper securely over the mouth of it, only perforating the paper with a pin to give the wrigglers air. In a day or two they will be surprised to see how many fullfledged mosquitoes there are on top of the water. In this way, little by little, it will dawn on them, that you are right after all, when you say that the little wrigglers turn into mosquitoes.

Next, you protect yourself against the onslaught of this

little foe, by sleeping under a curtain. To each bed there is a framework about three feet high, on which you stretch your mosquito net. With the net well tucked in about you, there is very little chance for him to get at you He will sing and drone and buzz around and blunder against the curtain until he gets tired, then he will sit down on the curtain-poles and sulk.

Someone has said, that if the Hindu doctrine about the transmigration of the soul is correct, the Indian mosquito must originally have been a Scotchman. The droning is unmistakably a survival of the bagpipe. And besides that you can trace the national shrewdness in his business methods, for having treated you to his music, he will next claim a "wee bit of a drappie."

If the mosquitoes have succeeded in filling your blood with the germs of malaria, there is yet one weapon left you—quinine. You eat it in powders, drink it in solutions, and swallow it made up into pills, and if that does not help, you are invalided home.

The flea is another enemy you have to deal with. In one way he is more to be feared than the mosquito, for he spreads the plague. In the crowded bazars and native houses, there are always a lot of rats. On these rats the flea lives and thrives. Now, rats are subject to the plague. When a rat gets the plague and dies, the fleas will leave the dead body, and likely as not go and bite a human being next and in that way transfer the plague.

War is therefore waged against the rats, but it is no easy matter to exterminate them, where one has to deal with narrowminded, fanatical Hindus, who shield the rat under the plea that all life is sacred. And when they believe that the spirit of some of their ancestors have come back to live with them in the body of a rat, you cannot reasonably expect much assistance from them in their extermination.

Among the Santals rats are not very safe. Roasted rat is a delicacy much coveted, especially by Santal boys.

There is yet another dangerous member of the bug family which ought to come in for some consideration. To mention his name would perhaps not be polite, so we shall speak of him as the B-flat bug. His home is preferably the cracks and joints of the native's bedstead, or in the floor mats, where people sleep, and his food is human blood.

For some time scientists have suspected Mr. B-flat, and now they have proved their case. They have found him guilty of transferring the germs of leprosy from one person to another. Everywhere in this land there are lepers. They often travel about from place to place exhibiting their horrid sores and stumpy hands and feet, while begging for alms. People pity them, give them food and shelter, often giving them one of their beds or mats to sleep on. Perhaps after the lapse of several years it becomes known, that some member of the charitable family has contracted the dreaded disease. The bug, having fed on the body of the leper, next bites someone, who has not got the disease, transferring the germs to him.

LEOPARDS.

Old Santals can tell us about the time, when the greatest part of Santalistan was covered with dense jungle, which was the home of tigers, leopards, bears, wild boar, buffaloes, elephants, deer and other animals. The Santals are both by profession and inclination clearers of jungle, grubbers and diggers. They started to clear the forest, and the fight began. The royal keeper of the jungle, the Bengal tiger, would not surrender his home and haunts without a fight. Many and weird are the stories told in the threshing-places of an evening about this fight. His royal highness was beaten. The long ironheaded arrows and spears as well as the traps of the alert conquerer of the jungle proved too much for him, he had to retreat.

Once in a while even now-a-days a tiger may stray into the district, but they are not at all common. However, the caves, where the oldtime man-eaters used to reside, are to be seen until this day. At the mouth of one cave I turned over the remains of two human skulls, ghastly souvenirs, which went to prove that the famous man-eating monsters, of whom the Santals tell such legendary tales, were not entirely mythical.

But I was going to tell about the leopards. They are relatives of the tiger, but there is no royal blood in their veins, that is certain. Compared with the tiger, they are lowbred, narrowminded and sneaky animals. They have made their home in the rocky hills and patches of jungle about us. At night they prowl about the villages and carry

SANTAL ARCHER.

away dogs, goats and even pigs. Yes, they do not even draw the line at a longlegged, razorback, brushbristle factory of a Santal pig. But their favorite dish seems to be the ordinary pariah dog. In the villages about Gombro hill there is hardly a yellow dog left to yelp at the moon. The leopards have eaten them all. And if you judge them according to the rule: "Tell me what you eat and I will tell you who you are," the leopards would not get very high marks on the character rolls.

In a year's time no less than four leopards were killed near our Kaerabani station. Two of our Christian workers are responsible for the death of one.

Early one morning I heard a man's voice at my door calling excitedly: "Saheb, lend us your rifle!"

The man was so excited and out of breath from running that he could hardly answer my question as to why he wanted the rifle. But at last I found out that a leopard had been located in a little patch of jungle near his village. I gave the man an old army rifle we had at the station, a few cartridges, and some good advice, and off he went at a gallop. I also sent off another hunter with a shotgun and bullets.

About noon I saw a long procession of people coming up the road towards the Mission. In the van was the dead leopard suspended from a bamboo pole carried by two sturdy Santals. Then came the two hunters with their guns. Following them were all the small boys within the radius of several miles, all talking and gesticulating, and evidently, discussing the events of the hunt.

There was the "big pussy," as the Santals called it, with a large bullet hole in it's forehead and another in it's shoulder. It was a young male leopard, measuring a little more than six feet from tip of nose to tip of tail. The old Snyder rifle in the hands of Boroda had done the job well. The leopard had taken refuge in a cleft between two rocks. The first shot broke it's shoulder and as it was about to drag itself out another bullet in the forehead ended its earthly career.

The people from the nearest villages soon gathered to

BORODA'S BIG PUSSY.

get a look at the dead "pussy." Some of them brought their small children, and though they screamed from fright, yet they were made to touch the dead animal. The Santals have a superstition that if a child is fussy and cries at night the best cure for it is to make it touch a leopard or any other ferocious animal. The leopard skin was given to me, and the Santals had a feast on the flesh.

Another time the same men got the rifle and went out and shot a striped hyena near the Mission station. A family of those so called scavengers of the desert had taken up their abode in a cave near by. When the head of the family was killed the others soon disappeared. The Santals ate the flesh of the hyena, also. And when I chaffed them about their appetites they told me that the flesh was fat and nice and made an excellent curry.

The Santals love to hunt. Very few of them, however, have guns. A native cannot keep a gun without first getting a license from the government. If a gun is found in the possession of a native, who has no license, he is promptly arrested, fined or imprisoned, and his gun is taken away from him. But if they have no guns they have bows and arrows and ironheaded spears, and many a wild beast of the jungle has fallen before these weapons. From childhood the Santal boys are taught the use of bows and arrows. They are among the few playthings a Santal boy possesses, and he uses them diligently. As soon as he is big enough to run about he shoots lizards and small birds and soon becomes a skilled marksman.

People often complain that there are but few song-birds in the Santal country, which is quite true. Birds of all kinds are very scarce, especially in the Santal villages. If one goes to a Hindu village one will at once notice the difference; there the trees are full of songsters, while in a Santal village even the chirp of a sparrow is rare. For this state of affairs the young Santal hunter, I am afraid, must bear the blame.

The Santals can tell many a "tall story" of leopard hunts, every one of them, they assure us, being as true as true can be. Here is a fair sample.

A LUCKY SHOT.

Near some villages about a days march from here, there lived some time ago a man-eating leopard. When a leopard once tastes human flesh and blood, he will eat nothing else. Among the victims of this leopard was the daughter of a village chief. On hearing this the people of the neighborhood were deeply stirred, and when the chief called for volunteers to help him hunt the leopard, a large number of young men came forward. Together with the chief they went out determined to kill the monster.

From early morning they beat the jungle, but they saw no sign of the animal. Late in the afternoon the village chief in some way became separated from his followers and wandered about alone. Suddenly he stood almost face to face with his enemy. Quick as thought an iron-pointed, reed arrow was fitted to the bowstring, a twang was heard and the arrow went into the shoulder of the animal. The wounded brute, now furious from pain, at once sprang at the chief. The latter dropped his bow and shinned up the nearest sal tree. But the tree happened to be a small one and being young and supple it began to bend over as he neared the top.

When the chief realized the situation he said to the leopard: "A few days ago you ate my daughter, and today it looks as if you will eat me."

He then jumped to the ground and the leopard began to chase him around the tree. Fortunately the chief got hold of the leopard's tail and saved himself by always keeping the tree between himself and the furious animal, all the time shouting for help.

When his hunting comrades at last arrived both the leopard and the chief were thoroughly exhausted. The animal was killed, but the skin was spoiled because most of the hair was worn off from the tail by the rubbing it had received against the rough bark of the tree.

Once we had a magistrate in the district, who was a keen hunter. He asked that word might be sent him if leopards were heard of in the neighborhood. A few days afterwards I had occasion to do so. The next morning out he came bringing with him two more Europeans and a few extra rifles. From the nearest villages I had secured some beaters, who brought with them several big drums and a number of dogs.

The magistrate arranged the hunt. The beaters were to start their beating in one end of the jungle in such a manner that the leopard when running away from them would not have to go against the sun. Being of the cat family the leopard prefers to go away from the sun rather than against it.

Rifles.and munition were then distributed and each of us Europeans were assigned places along the brow of the hill on the course which the leopard was expected to take, when the hunt began. Each one of us had a few Santals with him.

At a given signal the hunt began. Drums were beating, the Santals were shouting, their dogs were barking,—in short pandemonium broke loose. There was noise enough to frighten even the proverbial dead donkey. The narrow belt of jungle in which we were stationed was so dense that any animal smaller than an elephant could easily have passed within a hundred feet of us without being noticed.

The beaters were slowly coming down our way. We were all alert, gun, spear, arrow or stick in hand ready to give an account of ourselves should the leopard come our way. Ten minutes passed, fifteen minutes passed. The thing was beginning to get tedious, I thought. Then all of a sudden a Santal in front of me grew rigid. He turned an intensely drawn and fierce face toward me and whispered: "He is near us." We renewed our vigils and strained both eye and ear, but a regiment of leopards might well have passed us unobserved in that dense jungle.

After a reasonable pause I asked the man, how he could tell that the leopard was near. He replied: "I felt it in my body, every hair on my body rose and I felt that the animal was near us. It must have passed down this way." Then he led us into the jungle and showed us a few claw-marks, a broken twig, and a crushed leaf, as proof positive that the leopard had passed unchallenged within thirty yards of us.

The Santals are sons of the jungle and live nearer na-

THE CHURCH LEOPARD.

ture than we do, hence this strange sixth sence of feeling the nearness of an enemy befor seeing or hearing it.

But the most exciting leopard hunt we have had happened at Benagaria, the old head station of our mission. One morning a young man came and told us that he had seen a suspicious looking animal in a culvert by the big water reservoir, or tank, as it is commonly called. He thought it was a leopard. This we could not believe as those animals very seldom come into this neighborhood, but thought it must be a hyena, or perhaps a jackel, the man had seen. But to make sure we went over and had a peek into the hole. And true enough, there lay a leopard glaring at us from out of the semi-darkness of the culvert. Its eyes looked like two burning coals, and as we were unarmed we thought it best to keep at a safe distance.

All the available weapons at the mission consisted of an old pistol and a double barrel shot gun of which one of the barrels was cracked and useless. It was clear that if the leopard was to be killed it would have to be done by strategy. If we shot at it and wounded it someone would be sure to be either mauled or killed by it, as a wounded leopard is one of the most dangerous animals to have to deal with.

Quite a number of men gathered and we held a council of war. After discussing the pros and cons, public opinion seemed to concur in that drowning would be both as safe and painless a death as we could think of for the leopard.

The hole or culvert in which the animal had taken refuge is an opening about three feet high and the same width, running through an earth embankment, which is over fifty feet wide. The outer end of the culvert we decided to block up with an old door, and at the other end which comes out a couple of feet above the water of the reservoir we would place a large, strong fish-net. The plan was to get Mr. Spots to leave his refuge by the back door, get tangled up in the net and dragged into the water, where we thought we could dispatch him in ease and comfort.

People were gathering fast. How they found out that a hunt was on, I do not know. But within an hour there must have been about a hundred men present, all of them more or less excited over the prospect of a real hunt. Some of them had spears, some had stout sticks, but many had no weapons of any kind. The old pistol and gun were then loaded and given to the sharpshooters, the net brought forth and everything got into shape. First the outer entrance was blocked, then the net was spread before the inner opening and the signal given for a vigorous drumming at the old door to frighten the animal out the way we wanted it to come.

Everybody was now trembling with excitement, the nervous strain was awful. Suddenly a low growl was heard and a large head protruded from the culvert exhibiting a splendid set of teeth. The half a dozen or more who were holding the net dropped it and ran up the bank as fast as their legs could carry them. One look at that white dinner-set in the head of the leopard was enough for them. The way being clear the leopard walked leisurely over the net and up the bank to look for another hiding place. Fortunately the man with the gun did not fire and the animal trotted leisurely along towards an old limekiln. On closer inspection it was evidently not satisfied with the place as a refuge for one whose life was in danger, so it made for the church.

Whether it was instinct or some other and deeper reason which prompted the hunted leapord to look upon the mission church as a safe refuge is a question which could be discussed in another chapter. The fact is that it went straight to the church and jumped on to the veranda on the north side and began to look for an open door. But all the doors were closed. We saw what it wanted and sent a man around to the other side to open a door for it. This being done, we slowly persuaded it to proceed around to the south side, where it spied the open door, and the darkness inside was an invitation to it to enter. The door was at once closed and bolted and we started to take pot shots at it through the "jilmils" of the doors. On being wounded it roared furiously. Never has such a powerful voice been heard in the Benagaria church.

A HUNT.

The church proved to be a very poor refuge for the leopard, but an ideal place for the hunters. Someone was pumping buckshot into it all the time. Finally it went behind the organ and lay down and one of our carpenters, a Santal, Makai by name, got a chance to send a bullet through its neck which finished it. But in its death agony it bit large pieces out of the woodwork of the organ.

It was an old male leopard which measured seven feet from tip to tip. All day it lay on exhibition, and the whole neighborhood turned out to have a look at it. Old medicinemen begged with moist eyes that they might get leave to take away a few hairs from the leopards whiskers, from which to make a charm for some of their sick friends.

THE VILLAGE WHEELWRIGHT.

SNAKES.

India is a great country for snakes. It is said that the snake family is represented here by more than two hundred distinct species. Fortunately they are not all poisonous. Only thirty three kinds are dangerous to life, the chief among which is the cobra.

The cobra is not a very large snake. It is seldom in this district more than three and a half feet long, but it is a vicious brute. It does not flee from its natural enemy, man, but is ever willing and ready to fight. It is a horrid sight to see an angry cobra curled up, its raised head swaying from side to side, hissing, ready to strike a death blow at its enemy. One remembers that this little reptile yearly murders thousands and thousands of people.

When angry, the cobra expands the skin of its neck until it appears like a hood. On this hood are to be traced two round or oblong rings that look like a pair of spectacles. The hiss of the cobra is not unlike that of a goose. In the upper jaw, well forward, it has two sharp poisonous fangs. They are constructed so that they fold back when not in use; they are hollow and a small duct leads up from them to the poison glands in the cheeks. When the creature is angry, the fangs are erected and it strikes forward, puncturing the skin of its victim and injecting the poison. When bitten by a cobra a strong man will only live for an hour or two, so powerful is the poison.

SNAKE CHARMER.

The first cobra victim I saw was a young Mohammedan woman. She was standing beside the wall of her house when a cobra darted out of a hole and bit her. At once she called her people and told them what had happened, and with as little delay as possible they brought her to the native doctor at the mission only half a mile away. Within a few minutes after she was bitten she was so weak that she had to be carried. The doctor gave her a snakebite remedy and ordered her to be walked about and excercised so as to keep up her circulation. The poison attacks the involuntary muscles.

Some men dug the cobra out and brought it also to the mission. It was nearly four feet long and everyone who saw it declared it to be the largest cobra they had ever seen.

In spite of all the remedies the woman gradually grew weaker. Her legs became quite paralyzed and she was unable to move. The doctor said there was no hope for her, yet he did not give up, but had people help him to rub her arms and legs, nevertheless she sank gradually and within an hour she was dead.

When she was lying on the ground unconscious and the doctor had given her up, some Mohammedan women, her friends and relatives, broke small branches from a tree near by, squatted about the dying woman, and began to draw these branches down her body all the time repeating incantations. I asked the doctor what they were doing. He shrugged his shoulder and said:

They are saying "mantras."

Why do they say "mantras?"

With another shrug of shoulder he answered: "These people are very superstitious and think that "mantras" or incantations can save her life."

How sad to see their helplessness! Nothing but empty incantations to put against the potent poison of the cobra.

All cases of snakebite do not, however, terminate fatally. While at Kaerabani we had several which were all saved. I must tell you about one or two of them.

The Jarta family in the nearest village had decided to leave their "Bongas" and become Christians. They had received instruction and the day of their baptism had been fixed. We were all looking forward to the day when we could welcome them as members of the church.

On Saturday afternoon, the day before the baptism was to take place, while I was having a language lesson in the veranda, a young lad came up and told us that Jarta's wife had been bitten by a snake, that she was unconscious and had been carried to the house of the village headman, who was a heathen.

We started at once for the headman's house about half a mile away. When we reached it we found the poor woman unconscious, her feet and hands were cold, her pulse very faint and her breathing was very slow. Three or four women were sitting about her with twigs in their hands saying "mantras" and weeping. They were all heathen. I had brought a lancet and some permanganate of potash to rub into the place where the snake had bitten her, but we could not find the wound, and the woman in her unconscious state was, of course, unable to tell us. So we decided to take her to the mission house and try some other remedies which we had. We then lifted her on to a Santal bedstead and four men carried her to the mission bungalow. We ran the greatest part of the way against a heavy shower of rain, for it was in the rainy season, and when we reached the bungalow we were all as wet as we could be.

As we ran we laid the case before the Lord. If the woman should die, the heathen in the neighborhood would say that the "Bongas" or evil spirits had killed her because she was about to become a Christian. And the result would be that many, who were under conviction, and who were almost persuaded, would perhaps draw back and be lost to the Kingdom.

Humanly speaking there was little hope for the woman but we put the case in God's hand and determined to work as long as there were any signs of life.

Her mouth had to be forced open to get the medicine in, and by manipulating her throat she was made to swallow it. We rubbed her limbs, tried to restore respiration, and put hot water bottles about her, all the time calling on the Healer of man to raise her up. Several heathen neighbors from the village were there watching us, wondering what would happen. I cannot explain how eagerly we looked for signs of life. We must have worked a quarter of an hour with her when we noticed that her pulse was getting stronger, and, as we placed a hot water bottle against her back, she winced and groaned. A few minutes later she opened her eyes, gazed about her in a half dazed way, then stretching out her arms she said: "Where is my baby?" The victory was won. In a short time she was able to walk about. Our hearts were overflowing with praise and thanksgiving.

She was able to tell us afterwards that she went out to cut broom grass, and as she was working a cobra darted out and bit her foot. At once she started for the mission, but after running a little ways she got so faint, that she had to sit down. Fortunately there were some shepherd boys near by, to whom she could tell what had happened before she lost consciousness. One of those boys came and told us.

The next morning she was able to come to church and, standing beside her husband and children before the congregation, she confessed her faith in God and with her family received holy baptism. It was indeed a day of rejoicing for the little mission congregation.

About a year later a Christian woman from the same village was carried to our house. She had been found unconscious under a tree. We at once suspected snake poison and began to treat her in the same way as Jarta's wife. When she regained consciousness she told us that a cobra had darted out from its hole among the roots of the tree and with a vicious hiss had struck her. She at once gave herself up for lost, committed her soul to her Maker, and fainted away. Her little daughter playing near by, noticed that something was the matter with her mother, at once ran home to tell her big brother. With as little delay as possible the young man got help to bring her to the mission. After a few hours the woman was able to walk home, leaning on her son, but it took her several days to get over the effects of the poison.

Some time later I had another snake experience which I shall not forget very soon. Together with several of our native preachers I was doing evangelistic work in a district about ten miles to the north of our mission station. We were staying at a Government rest-house. It was in March and the weather was beginning to get hot, and the mosquitoes were very troublesome. In the evening I put my bed in the center of the room and left the doors on both sides open to get the benefit of whatever draught there might be. Beside my bed was a table on which were some tin cans and dishes. Two servants were sleeping on the veranda. They had their sticks with them. In fact when out in camp the Santals have a practice of going to bed with their sticks. There are snakes and scorpions, jackals and pariah dogs about, and a weapon may be required at any time.

About three o'clock in the morning I was awakened by a scraping, rasping noise among the tin cans on the table. There was a lantern in the room, but the light was turned down very low. In the dim light I thought I saw something resembling a rope stretched from one tin can to another within easy reach of my hand. I got the lantern, turned up the light, and there instead of a rope was a large snake. fixing me with his cold, beady eyes.

I called for my men with their sticks and between us we soon dispatched the snake, and that without breaking a single dish. It was not a cobra but was a so-called "kharite," a tree snake, very poisonous but not so quick to strike as a cobra. The snake had evidently been looking for a way to get into the thatch of the roof where a lot of sparrows had taken up their abode, and in order to get on to the table it must have climbed up the bedpost right by my head. No more sleep that night!

Tobacco acts on the cobra something in the same way that it's poison acts on a human being. Once I gave a cobra a tap on its head with my stick and stunned it. Then I asked a Santal for a little tobacco. This I put in the cleft of a stick and thrust it into the mouth of the angry snake and then let him go. At once he spread his hood, hissed and raised his head and we all kept at a safe distance. But it didn't last long, soon he seemed to get drowsy. His head came down, and he acted as if he were drunk. No amount of teasing would arouse him. Finally we pronounced him dead.

I said to the Santals: Now you can see what a great poison tobacco is that it kills even a cobra.

Quite a crowd had gathered to watch the performance and someone made the remark that the cobra was perhaps only drunk from the effects of the tobacco, and that it would come to life again. So we put the snake in an old earthen pot and covered it up, and the next morning there was no doubt that the cobra was dead "for good and always." Since then we have tried the tobacco experiment several times and it always works out the same way. Tobacco is poison for the cobra.

The natives are very much afraid of cobras, and well they may be, for their bare feet and legs make an easy target for the poisonous fangs of the snake. When out at night people often carry long sticks with which they beat the road in front of them. In that way they mean to frighten away any snake which may be about.

Once we had a Mohammedan living in our compound. He was a Sheik and thought himself a very brave man, afraid of nothing under the sun. Early one morning I saw him throwing stones and brickbats in through the open door of his house, all the time shouting at the top of his voice. At first I thought he had lost what little reason he had, and was running amuck, but finally I distinguished the word "sap," which means snake, and went over to see what was up. There in a corner of the man's room was a large cobra with hood expanded hissing away ready for business. A good whack across his neck soon settled him and he was brought out hanging limp from my stick. The Sheik salaamed and said: "The Saheb knows mantras."

During the hot weather snake-charmers often come to show us their pets and to make them "dance" for us as they express it. They carry their pets about in small, covered baskets. When they want to give an exhibition they squat on the ground and place the baskets in a row in front of them. Then they beat a little rattledrum and play some weird music on an instrument made from gourd. One by one the covers are then removed and the cobras raise their hooded heads and sway from side to side, or bob up and down while the snake-charmer and his assistant "make music." Of course the men are careful to remove the fangs from the poisonous snakes before taking them out to exhibit.

Sometimes they carry about with them great pythons

THE SNAKE CHARMER.

more than ten feet long and wind them about their necks and bodies.

In Benares one day we saw a snake that looked as if it had a head at both ends. The Hindus call it the two-headed snake, but on closer examination it appears that one of the heads is only a blunt tail.

THE RAINS.

The rains are supposed to make their appearance about the middle of June every year, and last in this district until the middle of September. Why it is called "rains" and not simply "rain" no one can explain, but after spending a rainy season or two in this country you will ask no questions, but think the designation quite proper.

For a couple of months before the rains set in it is very hot and dry. So dry in fact that the ground cracks. The sun beats down from a brazen cloudless sky scorching everything. The leaves shrivel up and fall like after a frost at home. And all living things suffer. Even the crow has nothing much to say, but hops about gaping ridiculously. And anything that can silence the Indian crow is not likely to be a fake, that is certain.

Yellow pariah dogs hop about on three legs resting one at the time from the scorching heat of the road. And dust is thick everywhere. Then it is that people travel by night and get under a shelter before the sun has passed one fourth of the sky.

About this time one begins to get interested in the weekly weather report of the government meteorological department to see if they have located the monsoon or not, and if they have, how far up it has got. It is to come up through the Bay of Bengal and bring new life to scorched and thirsty millions.

Before the rains set in we sometimes get thunder-

PLOWING.

storms. They usually come on in the afternoon and from the west. First a black cloud is seen overhanging the western sky. As it draws nearer it changes color. First gray then yellow, then purple. The rumbling of thunder is heard. In a few minutes the landscape is blotted out. Dust, dead leaves, more dust flies about you, envelopes you, and gets into your eyes and nose. Trees are blown over, thatch torn from the roof. All doors and shutters are closed. It is dark, almost like night. The storm howls. Blinding flashes of lightning pierce the dusty gloom. The very foundations of the house quake from the claps of thunder.

The result of this tremendous uproar may be only a few scattered drops of rain, or it may be a hailstorm accompanied by a copious downpour filling the dried up tanks and water courses, strewing the compound with leaves and debris, but relieving the heat for a few days. However this is not the "rains."

They come on the fifteenth of June. A soft wind from the south east swishes through the palms. White clouds come up. A drizzle falls upon the parched ground. More clouds hurry across the sky to bring relief to all living beings. It rains and rains. The mailrunner brings the newspaper. It is soaked, but you read with satisfaction the broad headlines: "The Monsoon has burst."

In a day or two the bare sunbaked ground is transformed. Green, green everywhere. The fireflies dart in and out among the tender leaves of the teak and tamerind trees. The gold mohar tree is ablaze with red flowers. Everything is throbbing with life.

Frogs croak everywhere. Some of them bray like goats. The crow has found its voice and caws with impunity.

The Santal puts away his superfluous clothes, oils his skin, gets his plow out and repairs it and looks as if he is going to get busy. Even the laziest of the lazy seems to have gotten some energy. It is the influence of the rainy season on the sons of the soil.

Too much spoils everything. Rain all day, rain all night. You are longing for a glimpse of the sun, because you want to set your clock right, but it persists in hiding itself and you feel lonesome for it.

Damp and wet all over, everywhere. No dry clothes to put on. They are all damp. Your pillow is damp. Your furniture seems to perspire. Your shoes — well you remember distinctly that they were black yesterday — today they are nearly white, covered with mould.

PLOWING.

Then one morning the sun comes out gloriously bright. Then is your opportunity to get your rooms and clothes dried.

From misty morning til evening dusk everybody is busy in the fields. First the embankments between the ricefields must be repaired so the water will stay in them. Then the water-covered field is plowed two or three times with a little wooden plow drawn by a pair of humpbacked oxen. When the field is ready, the little rice shoots are brought and set out by the women wallowing knee deep in the mud. Soon field after field is planted, turns dark green as the shoots take root and grow. The landscape is transformed. The desert is truly blossoming.

A REAPER.

About the steaming hot nights, the mosquitoes and the tired feeling you do not wish to talk. You feel you are a foreigner because the rains do not infuse you with energy. It is rather the other way. You do not want to admit that you get lazy, but you observe in yourself a strange disinclination to work. You want a long chair under the swinging panka where you can lie back in comfort and dream of the old homestead way out on the western prairies of God's country. You close your eyes and see it. A cool breeze fans your cheek, light fleecy clouds chase each other across the deep blue Minnesota sky. The wheat-fields look like a billowy sea. The air is full of the breath of new-mown hay. You dream.

"Saheb, they have brought a girl with a broken arm," says a soft voice beside you. It startles you. You have not heard the footsteps of your servant as he came to tell you. You were far away. Dreams aside, now it is work.

SCENE FROM KAERABANI.

A NIGHT IN A DAK BUNGALOW.

It is Hindustan, and evening, and a lonesome Dak bungalow or government rest-house by the side of a long and dusty road. The sun has just set across the hazy hills in eastern Chota Nagpore. Such a sunset! An Oriental sunset! As the yellow disc descended behind the hilltops it drew before its mysterious exit a curtain of glowing red. A few moments its gauzy web hung over the western sky; soon it softened into saffron, which again slowly yielded to prosaic gray.

Then came the short truce between light and darkness—which men call twilight — the "Hinterland" of day, the borderland between the world of deeds and the world of dreams.

The new moon outlines its silvery sickle against the background of gathering gloom.

From the native quarters behind the bungalow the elders and teachers are chanting sleepily. It is one of those weird chants which for the western ear possesses no melody save the melody of infinite sadness. It is one of the old Santal chants, to which Christian words have been composed. To the ear of a novice the tunes are nearly all alike. And not only those of the Santals, but also those of the other natives of the land, as well. The words and meter may vary, but the cadence in the main is the same. — It is the song of Hindustan—the dirge of one lamenting his long-departed youth and its divine illusions.

A LONELY BUNGALOW.

If you listen a while to that song, so spiritless and tuneless and endless, you can hear the servitude of millions, of myriads of men and women who have learned in suffering something which they try to teach in song. The essence of centuries of longings and heartaches and frustrated hopes is trying to find expression in one dreamy, plaintive refrain.

But night is here. You walk forth and back on the veranda while your servant is trying to set your supper-table on an upturned grocery box.

The sounds of day are hushed and the voices of the night are heard. The moon is disappearing. The blades of yonder palm are silhouetted against the starry sky, blades as delicately curved as the edge of a scimitar. Among the branches of the mango trees a few fireflies gleam intermittently, illuminating nothing but themselves. And the cricket sings. This is a land where the cricket chirps through all the year, and his song is melancholy, plaintive and dreamy, like the song of the other natives of the land.

In the solitude of the hot, sleepless nights the cricket is your companion and counselor. How intimate his song can grow, You read into those monotonous strains all your emotions until you cease to have any. Tch, tch, tch! It sounds as if it had been ringing from the beginning of time and was destined to go on ringing to the end.

At first it irritates you, then it depresses; but in the end it dominates you. Struggle as you will, you are doomed to succumb to its soothing strains. Tch, tch, tch! Night after night, it seems to din into your ear the essence of eternal monotony.

But the crickets are not your only companions and counselors. They only bring the refrain to the music of the unseen world.

Your eye as well as your ear is subject to the spell of night. The moon has now disappeared and there is the march of the stars, — a mighty host, ever moving onward, slow, solemn and silently eloquent. Here they scintillate in companies, there they shine in awful isolation. Some burn with a steady, penetrating brilliance, which seems to pierce your very soul, others twinkle, as it were.

in unison with the notes of the cricket. The song of the universe, the music of the spheres —let them call it what they will — but the spell of the night is upon you — and the spell of the mysterious East.

"Khana Saheb!" calls you back to things terrestrial. On your box is your curry and rice, the food of the East. A few years in Bengal have taught you to like it. Now you want it hot with pepper and other condiments, — again the influence of the East.

The Christian workers gather. You discuss the work of the day with them and at last commit yourself and them into the hands of Him who sleepeth not.

Your "charpoi" palmetto mat and blankets are ready. With a "johar," the servant disappears into the night. You are alone with your own thoughts — and the crickets. You turn the light of the lantern low, and as you do so the trade mark on the lantern chimney catches your eye. You read the words: "Made in Austria."

"Made in Austria — made in Austria" — The cricket takes up the words and fits them into his notes and chirps them into your soul. You try to rid yourself of them, but you cannot; you are under his spell. You want him to say "America" and not "Austria," but he persists. At last you give up and say: "What's the difference, Austria or America? it is exotic, foreign, anyway. Let it go with "Austria." Finally his song seems to grow fainter and fainter. From the far away distance is wafted back to you, from the the shores of the sea of stillness, faintly, very faintly, "Austria —A u s t r i a."

WITCHES.

The belief in witches and witchcraft is firmly rooted in the hearts and minds of the Santal. However, the Santals are not alone about this belief, it is common both among the Hindus and Mohammedans in this district. Almost daily the magistrates in our courts have to hear cases in which women are accused of witchcraft, or some trouble has arisen at the bottom of which this belief is to be found.

In their old "Sagas" or traditions the Santals tell us how it was brought about that they learned the craft.

"Once long, long ago the Santal men met together to discuss the question, what they ought to do with their wives. They were entirely out of hand and did not obey their husbands. When asked to do a thing, or on being corrected by their husbands as the head of the family, the women would turn around and abuse and scold them. And as everyone knows, when it comes to abuse, a man is no match for a woman. The men agreed to carry their grievances to Marang Buru, the devil, and ask his assistance.

At midnight they gathered in the sacred grove, called Marang Buru, and addressing him as grandfather laid their troubles before him. The old man very graciously consented to help them. He would give them occult power which would enable them to defend themselves against the wiles of their women. Before he granted them the power they would, however, have to make their signatures on his documents in their own blood. He gathered some leaves from a sacred tree and asked the men to draw blood and put their marks on the leaves. This frightened the men and they asked their grandfather to kindly excuse them for the time being, they would return the next night and sign the documents.

Unknown to the men some women had followed them to the grove and from their hiding place heard everything that was said. When they saw the men arise they hurried home by a short cut, and before the men arrived all the women in the village knew just exactly how the land lay.

The next day the men found a great change in their women-folks. They were as amiable and nice as they could be and the men began to think that it would not be necessary for them to sign Marang Burus documents. The next night they did not return to the grove as they had promised. On the following day the women were still more loving and kind to them, gave them extraordinary good things to eat, brewed rice beer and gave them so much of it that by night they were dead drunk.

This was the opportunity the women were looking for. They took their husbands clothes and turbans, pasted some goatshair on their upper lips and at midnight started for the sacred grove. After having saluted their grandfather they asked him to bring his leaves that they might sign them, for they could no longer endure the torments of their wives.

Marang Buru brought the leaves, the women pricked

their skins with thorns, pressed out a drop of blood and signed their husbands' marks on the leaves. Marang Buru then taught them witchcraft and gave them full directions how to "eat people." Before cock's crow they returned to their homes rejoicing.

After their debauch the men slept rather late the next morning and were not in the best of humor when they at last got about. They very soon found out that their women had not reformed after all. They were worse than ever. Again they had a consultation and decided to go that very night and put their marks on Marang Burus leaves.

When they told their grandfather what they wanted he was very much surprised and said: "I have already taught you. What more do you want?" But the men declared that they had not been near him since the first night when he asked them to sign and they promised that they would return the next night. Marang Buru, however, brought out the leaves and asked the men to see for themselves if it was their marks or not. They had to admit the marks but declared that they did not put them there.

When Marang Buru at last understood that the women had deceived both himself and their husbands he got into a great rage and swore that they would yet get even with those rascally women. He got some more leaves and asked the men to put their marks on them. This they did as directed and Marang Buru then set out to teach them the art of the Jan Guru, how to find out witches. And ever since that time there has been enmity between the witches and the Jan Guru.

The Santals believe that the witches have their meetings at night in some sacred grove or forest. When their husbands are asleep they get up, say some incantations and put a broom or some similar object in the bed beside them and the men, poor fools, feeling the broom beside them believe it to be their wives and have no idea of what is really going on.

It is also believed that witches do not walk on the ground, but by means of sorcery fly through the air in whatever direction they wish. The "Bongas" also appear to them and dance and flirt with them. They also play with tigers, ride on them, caress, and kiss them. These gambols they continue till nearly cock crow, when they return to their homes remove the broom and lie down in their proper places.

Witches make pupils of young girls. At night they go about from house to house and call for them. Then they take them to the sacred grove, teach them "mantras" and other things pertaining to the practice of witchcraft. If the girls are unwilling to learn they tell them that the tigers will eat them and thus frighten them into learning. When a pupil has advanced far enough they put her to a test by asking her to "eat" some one of her own relatives, her father, brother or sister. Should a pupil refuse to submit herself to this test the witches will make her ill or cause her to become demented or mad. Witches must feel no mercy for anybody, not even their own husbands and children.

It is very easy for the missionary to ridicule all this talk about witches and brand it as silly nonsense, but the fact still remains that to the Santals these things are actual and real.

The Bonga worship of the Santals is essentially a man's religion. Women have almost no place in it. Many of the sacrifices she may neither touch nor taste. For this reason it may be that the women may have felt a desire for some sort of worship of their own, that may account for their nightly gambols and offerings. That they possess any occult power by which they cause their victims to become sick and die is very improbable. There are plenty of herbs and roots which if given to anyone together with their food will cause sickness and death. Be that as it may, the fact remains that the belief in witchcraft is a superstition that dies hard. Every now and then a case will crop up among the Christians, where some poor woman is suspected of practicing witchcraft.

One morning a big Santal came up to me and asked me to look at his back and shoulders. One glance at his broad, brown back told me that he had been in a fight and had rather got the worst of it. He had received a good beating.

I knew the young man well, and instead of sympathizing with him told him that I was ashamed to see that he, a giant of a man, had let himself be licked. But my banter did not have the desired effect. The young man sat down and cried like a baby. He finally told us that his father had given him the beating. His father was a thin weazened old man whom one would not quickly suspect of such deeds.

"Why did your father beat you?"

"Because I would not send my wife away. How can I send her away now, we have three children; who will take care of them if I send her away?"

"But why should you send your wife away?"

Little by little the facts of the case came out. The old man and his four sons and their families live close together, and, as the custom is among the Santals, work their fields jointly and hold a good deal of the property in common. Except the oldest son and his family they are all Christians. Of late there has been a good deal of sickness in the family of the eldest son. One medicine man after the other had been called in without result. At last a medicine man greater than all the rest was called in and he succeeded in finding out what the trouble was why the medicine did not have any power to heal the sick ones. There was a witch at the bottom of the trouble. The help of a witch-finder was then sought. This dignitary after receiving his fee

A MEDICINE MAN.

led the suspicion towards the wife of the second son. He did not mention her by name but by hints and parables at which they are such adepts, gave the men to understand just exactly who was meant.

On returning from the witch-finder the old man took the case in his own hands. The suspected daughter-in-law was ordered to make the sick ones well at once. She protested that she was innocent. Then he ordered her to leave her house and family and never to show her face there again. On this he got his stick and proceeded to enforce his order at once. Then the son interfered with the result that he received a good beating.

We adviced the young man to go home and keep quiet for a few days, then we would take up the case and try to restore peace.

A week or two later we gathered the whole family and had a heart to heart talk with them. By that time the old man was thoroughly ashamed of what he had done and ready to sue for terms. We asked him to beg his daughter-in-law's forgiveness and to make her a present of a cloth. And for the offence he had caused in the church by running after witch-finders and believing in their humbug, he was asked to drop forty cents in the collection box for the poor.

THE JAN GURU.

He is a rather pleasant old man and fond of a joke. You will find him squatting on the sunny side of the village streets as you pass through. His name is Jarta, or rather that is the name he is known by. What his real name is, I do not know. Jarta means matted locks. For years and years, perhaps from the time he was a small boy. Jarta's hair has never been washed, combed or cut. It has been allowed to grow and has through the years gathered itself into four or five matted locks stiff with ancient dirt and oil. They look like pieces of dirty ropes hanging down his back or wound around his head.

If you look closely at his face you can tell that he is a cunning and crafty man. His small shifting eyes take in everything about you at a glance. And cunning and crafty he needs to be for he is a Jan Guru and that means a witch-finder.

Jarta is indeed a bad man and has caused a lot of mischief among his people. Yet he is very nice and polite and likes to talk to you, that is as long as you don't talk to him about his Savior and the salvation of his soul. As soon as that subject is broached he becomes quiet, and if you keep on he will get up and leave you; but he will never dispute or argue with you.

The heathen Santals believe firmly in witchcraft, and when they are sick they always fear that some witch is at the bottom of their trouble, and, as they express it, is eating

THE JAN GURU.

out their insides. Like everyone else a sick Santal wishes to get well as soon as possible, so he sends for an Ojha or medicine-man. That dignitary comes, feels the pulse of the sick one and shakes his head like a real doctor. He then goes out, collects the friends of the patient and gives them the result of his diagnosis. He has found the sick one in a very bad state indeed. It must be either "Bonga" or a witch that is causing the mischief. Do the friends wish him to find out for them?

"Yes, by all means!" they answer.

The Ojha then asks his fee. When that is secured he gets two leaves from the sal tree, puts a few drops of oil on them, rubs them against each other and from the marks the oil has made on the leaves pretends to read the cause of the sickness. If it is found to be a "Bonga" that is tormenting the victim, that personality must by means of offerings be persuaded to leave. If it is a witch, she must be found and brought to terms, and there is where the Jan Guru comes in. He alone can tell who the witch is that causes the trouble.

As soon as the relatives of the sick find out that it is a witch that is "eating" their friend they lose no time but prepare at once to go to some Jan Guru. A whole party will go, often one man from each house in the village. Their mission is a secret one and they will tell no one where they are going and often even get to their destination by a circuitous route. This is done to prevent evil spirits from putting obstacles in their way.

Arriving at the village of the Jan Guru, they usually have to wait a while before they get an audience. They must first send him presents and offerings. When they come before him he will ask a number of leading questions about the neighbors and relatives of the sick one, and he usually manages to get at what he wants without arousing the suspicions of the people who have come to him. He will find out, perhaps, that the wife of the sick man has been quarreling with some other woman in the village who has been found guilty of witchcraft before. He will settle on some one, and after certain ceremonies are gone through, he will begin to describe the house she lives in, her relation to the sick one and other things about her, so that although he names no one, everybody is sure of whom he means.

The most of the men went away suspecting just that woman, and now their suspicions are confirmed. With the Jan Guru it was a case of finding out just what advice was wanted and giving them that.

The Jan Guru may also have a tout or helper who will get into the confidence of the men, and having found out everything, bring word to his accomplice, sharing the profits.

The party now returns home and then trouble begins. The poor suspected women is dragged out and threatened with all sorts of violence, and if the sick one does not improve, they will carry out their threats. It is not uncommon that all this fuss togather with the assurance that the witch has really been discovered, has a restorative effect on the sick one, and he begins to feel better. If he does not improve, you may pity the poor witch.

A few years ago some people from a village six miles away came to Jarta with their troubles. The son of their headman was at death's door. After receiving his fee Jarta went into a trance and indicated who the witch was. The men went home and threatened her, but the boy did not improve. When he was dying they drove the poor woman out of the village and beat her so that she died from the treatment she received. Of course the offenders were put in prison for it. Old men will tell you that it was not at all uncommon in olden times to put witches to death. Now the usual thing is to drive them from their villages. Many a home has been broken up that way, and many a woman has had to leave husband and children and flee to her friends, if she had any, because she was accused of witchcraft.

The old Jan Guru knows he is a humbug but he won't leave off his evil practice because he makes an easy living by it.

A SACRED GROVE.

IN CAMP.

During the rainy season it is not possible for the missionary to do much village visiting. For one thing the mud is too deep in many places even for a horse to get through, and unless the missionary is bare of foot and leg, can walk the embankments between the flooded rice fields and wade through the brooks and mud, he will find it rather hard to get about. And besides, he will likely as not find the village empty of people when he gets there. Every man woman and child who is able to work will be busy in the fields. During this time of the year the native Christian workers go about from ricefield to ricefield and stop to speak a word to the busy plowmen or the women at work planting.

By the first of October the roads will be passable, the people at leisure, and the mornings cool and comfortable. Then, if you are a hustling missionary, you will get out into camp. You leave home for a week at the time and go to some of the out-stations of your district. The workers in charge of the station has been looking forward to your coming, and the place will be cleaned up spick and span. Usually there is a room for you to stay in, and you bring out with you a little furniture, such as a table, a chair and a bed. Of course to a jungle missionary these things are not absolutely necessary; you can get along with a mat on the floor for bed and squat on the floor when you take your meals. It is wonderful how many things you can get along without and yet be perfectly happy. One thing, however,

PLANTING RICE.

you had better not forget, and that is to bring your cook. You can not afford to take any chances with your stomach in this country.

If you have no mission out-station to go to, there is perhaps a Government Dak bungalow in which you can stay, while you work in the villages about. These bungalows or rest-houses are built by the government for magistrates and officers to stay in while on their tours of inspection in the districts. When not occupied by servants of the government, the meek and humble Padre Saheb is as a rule permitted to use them. Some of the bungalows are furnished and can be quite comfortable; but many of them consist only of an empty room or two with rows of large and small bats hanging from the rafters.

Apropos, a word about the bats. You abhor them at first when you see their little beady eyes glare at you by day, and at night, when you hear the flopping of their leathery wings close to your ear you do have sort of a creepy feeling, which is not exactly conducive to sleep. There is something uncanny and disagreeable about a bat. But little by little you get used to them, and at last you learn to love them. If you go to a bungalow, where here are no bats, you miss them. They are your friends. If a mosquito is buzzing about your unprotected forehead with evil intentions, one of your little friends will promptly come to your rescue, snatch up the mosquito and eat it. That is why you love them. At dusk you enjoy watching the erratic flight of the little ones as they take their flying lessons, and by the way catch a few moths and mosquitoes.

If there is no Dak bungalow to stay in and no out-station to go to, there is yet another way open to you if you want to get into camp. You can bring a tent. A good tent with a double roof can be quite comfortable, and you have the advantage that you can be near the villages and move about easily from place to place. There are usually a few spreading mango trees near the village under which you can pitch your tent.

After the first day or two camping is not so exceedingly interesting, but it is a means to a good end. That is why you keep it up. And when you speak of comforts, you do so relatively. There are degrees of comfort, as everyone knows.

A rich American lady, very much interested in missions and a liberal giver to the great cause, thought she would like to see for herself what a missionary's life was like. So she decided to come out to India for a few months. On the advice of the missionaries she came out during the cold season. She was met at the railway station and taken out to the nearest mission station and made as comfortable as possible. She visited around for some time and everybody did their best to make her stay as enjoyable as possible. When a lady missionary invited her to come out camping with her, she accepted the invitation eagerly.

The servants, the tents and camp outfit was sent out ahead and the ladies followed the next day. There were neither roads nor vehicles, so they were carried in "dandies." At dusk they arrived at the camp and found everything in order. They had only time for at little look around the place when the cook announced that dinner was ready. The table was set under a mango tree. There was no room for it in the tent. A lantern was suspended from a branch above the table. It was a perfect evening, cool and calm. The starry sky above, the mango tree with its fireflies and the silent Indian night perfectly fascinated the visitor. She was enraptured, charmed with everything.

"Why," she exclaimed, "everything is perfectly heavenly. How you missionaries can talk of sacrifices and discomforts I cannot understand."

The lady missionary smiled and kept her council. Fortunately no stinkbug found its way into the visitor's soup and no jackals howled just then. Dinner over they retired to the tent. There was a chair and a cot for each of them.

The visitor thought everything was "just charming." When they retired for the night the missionary brought in a stout stick and placed it beside her bed.

"What are you going to do with the stick?" the visitor asked.

"O it's handy to have to kill snakes with and drive out stray village dogs, and the like," answered the missionary.

"You don't mean to say that dogs and snakes can come in to our tent?" the visitor again anxiously inquired. The missionary lady then proceeded to enlighten her by relating some of her actual experiences with jackals, village dogs, snakes and scorpions. "Why, it was only the other day that I shook a large scorpion out of my shoe before putting it on in the morning. In fact we old Indians always shake our shoes before putting them on. It gets to be a habit with us."

Nothing awful, however, happened that night except that the visitors fine silk skirt slid off the chair where she had put it and laid on the ground completely ruined by white ants. Her shoes she had kept beside her on the cot. The next day was a busy one in camp. Sick people were brought and had to be helped. There were schools to be examined and meetings to be held. And besides that one of the servants while gathering firewood had been stung by a scorpion. He was in agonies the most of the day.

Again they had a lovely dinner under the mango trees, but it was not quite as charming as the previous. That night the visitor kept all her belongings with her on the cot. They had only but retired when the visitor screamed for help. "I am stung. It's my ankle! It's a scorpion! Help quick, auh!"

The missionary told her to lie perfectly still and she got the lantern which was left burning in the room, turned up the covering at the place where the wounded ankle was supposed to be. After a diligent search she found, not a dreadful scorpion, but a sharp toothpick which in some way had dropped into the bed.

Peace was again restored and the tired missionary was on the point dropping off to sleep when she heard a small

IN THE THRESHING PLACE.

voice calling her by name and inquiring if she was asleep. On being assured that she was awake the visitor said: "Did you hear me say last night that I thought missionaries ought not to talk about sacrifices, hardships and discomforts? Well, may the Lord forgive me. Goodnight!"

A few days or weeks of camp life will develope your taste for it, and if there are any discomforts or hardships you learn to take them as part of your days work. Together with your Christian workers you go out from your temporary home every morning to preach the gospel in the adjoining villages. The field is often one seldom visited by the preachers and there are no Christians in the neighborhood.

THRESHING RICE.

Early in the morning you go to the threshing places just outside the village. There is where you will find the people. Usually several threshing places lie close together, and often you can get a score of men who will sit for hours on the sunny side of a pile of straw and listen to the message of salvation.

The people are strangers to your Christian workers as well as to yourself and you must approach them carefully and tactfully if your visit is to do any good. It is best for you at first to keep in the background and like good children be seen rather than heard. You leave it to your preachers to establish proper relations. After a few com-

THRESHING RICE.

monplace remarks about the crops or the weather one of the preachers will say: "Den thamakur!" which means, "Give us some tobacco."

You may happen to know that the man who begged for tobacco has a good supply of that weed tied up in his cloth, but that does not prevent him from begging. Tobacco is used as a means of establishing polite and friendly relations between the Santals. If a man is unwilling to share his tobacco, there is very little use in trying to talk to him. Usually a dry tobacco leaf is forthcomming. The preacher takes it and gives it over to some young man in the gathering and asks him to prepare it. Squatting on the ground he will then proceed to rub the tobacco leaf to powder in

BRINGING HOME THE GRAIN.

the palm of his hand. He will then ask for "chun" or slacked lime. From the waistband of someone a folded leaf will be extracted and handed to the tobacco maker. In this leaf there is powdered lime burnt from clam shells. A little of the lime is sprinkled on the powdered tobacco and mixed well with it. When all is ready the tobacco maker will rise and if he is a devout worshipper of the

"Bongas" he will scatter a little pinch on the ground as an offering to them, and then he will go from one to the other of the party putting a little pinch of the powder into the right palm of each who wishes to partake. By a dexterous movement of the hand the men will manage to transfer the tobacco from the palm to their mouth without spilling a single grain and without the hand touching the lips.

Fortunately etiquette does not demand that the missionary should partake of the preparation. It would be rather hard on him if it did.

The tobacco has now broken the spell, coldness and reserve have melted away, tongues are loosened, ears and sometimes hearts are opened for the message of peace. You are permitted to sow the seed. Sometime, perhaps after many days, there will be a harvest.

AMONG THE BRETHREN.

The tent is pitched under some spreading matkom trees just outside the village. The hot, steamy and sultry days, which follow the rainy season, are over, and the air is delightful. It is autumn in Santalistan, and the sound of the sickle is heard in the rice-field.

There is a chair at the tent door, where you can sit and watch and listen. The shadows are growing long and the day is preparing its departure. With heavy sheaves on their heads, the women are returning from the rice fields. In spite of their heavy burdens they laugh and talk. The joy of the harvest is in their hearts. Another picture flashes across your mind:--the last great harvest and the songs of rejoicing of those, who are then able to bring in sheaves.

The shepherd boys are bringing the cattle, goats and sheep home toward the village. Slowly they amble along as if keeping time to the music of the bamboo flutes which the boys are playing. The mellow flute-notes quiver in the calm evening air. Long, trembling notes they are with an undercurrent of longing and sadness and hopelessness. Especially hopelessness, the sad hopelessness of one who has been oppressed and almost crushed, and only retaining the half faded memories of that which was and can never be again.

You listen and listen until you seem to enter into the spirit of that music and you think you understand it. That burden of sadness, which is borne to you on those trembling,

BRINGING IN THE SHEAVES.

minor flute-notes, is it not the essence of the life experience of the Santal people? Their history is that of an oppressed race, whose pride has never been entirely crushed. But repeated flights from oppressors, leaving ruined homes behind, to begin again life's struggle in other places must have spread a pall of hopelessness over them like the black smoke rising from their funeral pyres.

As a people they have been homeless, drifting from place to place, and they have been stunted like a tree often transplanted. There was nothing, which bound them to the soil they tilled and to the forests they hunted. Their dear ones died and were carried out to the burning ghat. From among the ashes of the funeral pyre a few charred bones were collected, not to be stored in sacred urns in their sanctuaries, but to be thrown into the Damukdia river. On the banks of this, their sacred stream, they were left standing alone with their burden of sorrow; the river carried away from their sight the last tangible vestige of connection between the living and the dead. The last sad duty to the departed one was performed. They looked into the mists of the broad river, but there was no joyful vision there, no hand outstretched to take away the burden of sorrow.

This is the feeling they have tried to express in their simple music. There may be thrills in those melodies which aim at gayety, but it is only for a moment, always, always the strains of sadness will return.

You can but think how different everything would have been if there had been a memory to cherish, a grave to keep green, or a sacred spot to defend.

You awake from your reverie to find that it is growing dusk. The weird music has ceased and the last stragglers of the herd have been brought in for the night. Rest and peace take the place of the busy hustle of the day. But for a lonely pigeon cooing from the copse the stillness is almost oppressive.

Out of the dusk, white-clad figures begin to appear. It is time for evening prayers. Slowly and in single file they come and squat on the greensward in front of the tent, men on one side and women on the other. It is a Christian village and the assembly for evening prayers is a large one.

Heartily they join in the singing of a hymn. The great majority of them are illiterate, but they have learned most of the hymns by heart, and with a strong voice to lead them they find no difficulty in following the words of the hymns. A portion of scripture is read and the old but ever new story of Jesus and his love is told again. The eye of faith is directed to look beyond these trancient and temporal things to those, which are real, everlasting and unchangeable, the love of God.

After prayers, ending with all repeating the Lord's prayer in unison, they say good-night. The women depart to prepare the evening meal, but the men linger. They say good-night but are in no hurry to depart.

Someone prepares tobacco, and with that for an excuse the men again sit down and draw their thin cotton sheets well up about their shoulders for the night air is cool. Little by little conversation becomes general. At first it is "small talk" about crops, cattle and the like, but finally it drifts into serious channels. Trouble and ill feeling between brethern is brought to light and discussed. Opinions for and against, are freely expressed. It is dark, no man's face can be seen distinctly, and that very fact seems to give them courage to express what is in their hearts.

Before long men are asking each other's forgiveness. Old troubles are settled. It is nearly midnight when someone suggests that we again surround the mercy-seat to offer thanks to Him, who is the author of love.

As you kneel that night beside your cot in your lonely tent, you feel mean and humbled because you so often have grumbled and complained as if the work was in vain and the days wasted. Now that you have seen the work of His spirit, you feel that you ought with all your heart to praise Him for calling you to be His witness among these grown-up children. As you confess your sins and try to claim His promises, and look up into His face, so full of love and tenderness, you can but say: "Had I a thousand lives to live, I should place them all on Thy altar to be dedicated to Thy service among these people."

THE HOUSE-BUILDERS.

IN DULU'S COURT-YARD.

Dulu was for a long time the only Christian in the village and has been the object of considerable persecution. Not that anyone did him bodily harm, for there are other ways of persecution. His heathen neighbors slighted him in every possible way, they could think of, and heaped all sorts of ridicule on him whenever they had an opportunity. But Dulu was not discouraged, neither did he become sour or bitter. He just smiled through it all. His life was a daily testimony for Christ among his benighted neighbors. And his testimony was not in vain, the tide turned and now about half of the villagers are Christians.

One day—it was before the tide had turned—we were having a meeting in a threshing place near Dulu's house, and after having tried to make the way of salvation as clear as possible, we called on those present to express their opinion. A young Santal stretched himself, yawned and said: "What do you gain by becoming a Christian? I can't see that it is any easier for you people to support yourselves that it is for us. We have to work for our living whether we are Christians or heathen."

To this question Dulu in his quiet way replied: "You all know that I came to this village together with my father when I was a boy ten or twelve years of age. My mother and sister had died in the famine and father and I came here in quest of work. A short time afterwards we became Christians. We were then as poor as we could be. All my earthly possessions was a stick. And today, though I am far from rich, yet my children need not go hungry and naked. Had I remained a heathen I should have been worse off than any of you. I do not work harder than the rest of you, neither do my fields yield more than yours. How is it that I have food and many of you have none? My friend, it is God's blessing and nothing else."

There was nothing to reply. Everyone knew that what Dulu said was true, and the man with the materialistic objection could only hang his head.

Dulu can not give long discourses on Christianity, nor preach, nor exhort, but he tries to live Christ, and after all that is what counts. That so many of his fellow villagers have turned to Christ is more due to the testimony of Dulu's life than to the preaching of the Christian workers.

One morning four preachers happened to meet in the village and after visiting the Christians we agreed to go to Dulu's house for a little rest and a drink of water. Dulu has four houses built in such a way that there is an open square or courtyard in the center. The house nearest to the street is the cowhouse. One end of this has been partitioned to the courtyard. The heavy door studded with iron and brass nails gave evidence of prosperity. Not many people in the village could afford such a door. As we entered, Dulu's wife at once brought out a couple of string beds for the preachers to sit on, and a small stool for the Saheb. Then she went and got a few brass vessels, filled them with water and put one on the ground before each of us, whereupon she made obeisance before each one in turn. Each one of the preachers received the kind of greeting his relationship to her entitled him to.

In the meantime Dulu appeared. He had been repairing a wall but climbed down, washed his hands and feet and came forward to greet us. After tobacco had been made and distributed, and the usual talk about health and crops got over with, Dulu remarked: "The Lord has been very good to us. We had a wonderful experience last night." He then told us the following story.

Dulu and his family had retired as usual the evening before. The children slept on a mat on the floor of the same room as their father and mother. In the corner of the room a number of chickens also spent the night huddled together. Chickens have free run of the bedrooms of the Santals and they never sit on a perch but huddle in a corner and early in the morning they rouse the family. The only alarm clock the Santal has is a cock.

During the night Dulu was awakened by the cackling of the chickens. He lit his lamp to see what was the matter an found two hens flopping around on the floor dying. The rest of the chickens were running about hiding here and there. At once he understood that a cobra had paid him a visit.

Dulu got his stick and began to search for the snake. All through the room he searched but could not find it. He roused his wife and children and they all joined in the search, but all in vain. They were all very much frightened. How could they lie down and go to sleep again knowing that the cobra might be hiding in the room? Dulu then set the lamp on the floor and asked his wife and children to kneel with him and pray that the Lord might show them where the snake was hidden.

When the prayer was ended Dulu looked up and there on the threshhold he saw the head of the cobra. It was returning to the room. A moment more and Dulu's stick de-

IN THE SHADE OF THE MATKOM TREE.

cended on its head and the danger was over. Again the family knelt on the floor, this time in thanksgiving for the wonderful deliverance.

"The Lord saw how frightened we were," said Dulu, "and He just sent that cobra back so I could kill it and we could all lie down again and rest safely until morning."

OUT OF THE DARKNESS.

Life everywhere has its ups and downs, its joys and sorrows, its days of sunshine and its days of darkness and gloom. The life of a missionary is no exception to this rule. There are days of disappointments, dark and gloomy days when dreams of victory vanish and it seems as if the enemy is gaining ground all along the fighting line.

At the time referred to in this sketch we had just passed through such an experience. Christians had fallen and would not let themselves be raised up again. Inquirers had come forward, but none of them seemed to get courage to take the step and confess their faith in Christ. Among our inquirers at this time, and of whom we entertained hope, was a Hindu belonging to one of the lower castes. He had shown great interest in the truth taught him, and had repeatedly expressed a desire to become a Christian. But when he was asked to take his stand for Christ and confess Him openly, he withdrew and for a couple of months we could not get near him. Our opportunity to talk to him was cut off, but not the opportunity to pray for him.

Daily this Hindu and his family were carried to the throne of grace by the little band of workers.

Suddenly one early morning in a pouring rain Puchu, for that was his name, came to the mission, sought out one of the workers and asked to be taken to the missionary. Something had happened to him, he said

AN OLD CHRISTIAN.

He began to explain that the reason why he had come now was that he wished to become a Christian and wanted to be baptized right away. On inquiring what had brought about this sudden change in him who only a short time before had declared that he would not break with his caste and become a follower of Christ, he told the following story.

After being convinced in his heart that Christianity was

right, his earnest desire was to become a Christian. He spoke of this to some of his friends, but they frightened him and told him that if he became a Christian he would be outcasted, no one would help him when sick or in want, and when he died, no one would take his body out to the burning ghat, but it would be left to rot in the house. They also threatened him with bodily violence if he broke caste. For these reasons he gave up the idea of becoming a Christian and kept out of the way of the preachers. When they came to his village he would hide somewhere rather than meet them.

The previous evening he had retired as usual and fell asleep. About midnight he awoke with the strange sensation that someone was in the room. He looked up, and there beside his bed stood a tall figure. At first it was indistinct and then gradually it became clearer until every detail of its form and face stood out very clearly. From the left arm of this strange visitor hung a long white robe, and although nothing was said Puchu understood that the robe was intended for him. A long time the visitor stood beside the bed. At last Puchu asked him: "Are you not going to give me that robe?" To this the visitor made no reply, but as Puchu looked up into his face he saw that he was weeping. A moment more and the strange visitor was gone.

Puchu could not sleep any more, but lay thinking about what this strange vision meant. And the more he thought, the clearer it seemed to him, that the white robe was the salvation, which he had refused to accept for fear of his caste fellows. God wished to give it to him, but he had refused it, and the messenger had wept because he had to take the robe away again. The thought also occurred to him that it was now too late to seek salvation, and that he was to die soon. What should he do?

At daybreak he got up, picked up his stick and his umbrella, and without saying a word to his wife came to the mission and wanted to be baptized at once.

We told him that both he and his family ought to be further instructed, and when prepared they would all receive baptism at the same time. But he would not be refused. He wanted to be baptized today, right away. He was convinced, that if he did not get baptized that very day he would die.

We saw that the man was deeply stirred and that it would perhaps not be well to postpone his baptism; so we sent him to bring his family. One of the Christian workers accompanied him. They returned with four of the children, his wife and eldest daughter were not as yet ready to follow him. Together with his children Puchu received baptism the same day. It was a day of rejoicing for us all, but especially for Puchu. His wife and daughter were instructed, and a month later we were able to welcome them also to the church. Years have passed since then, but we have never yet had reason to regret that we received Puchu as a candidate for baptism with but little previous instruction.

A short time after Puchu's conversion another soul was brought from out of the darkness in a similar way. She was an old blind woman over sixty years of age. Her daughter was the wife of one of our Christian workers and a warm-hearted woman. One day she came to the mission with a very sad and heavy heart. She had just returned from a visit to her old mother. After having told about her visit she burst into tears and said: "Every day for fifteen years I have been praying for my mother's conversion, but she seems farther away from God today than ever before. Today she scolded me and told me never to speak to her again about her soul. It seems as if the Lord will not hear my prayers, what shall I do?"

Looking at it from a human standpoint the hope for the old woman's conversion was not very bright. She was an exceptionally hard old heathen, well versed in all "Bonga" matters, and experience has taught us that such people seldom change, especially at her time of life. But we are not supposed to look at such cases from our standpoint, but from His, who is able to bring even those in the darkness of death back to life and light. God's promises were held up before the brokenhearted woman and she went away to keep on praying and trusting in God, that He would find some way of touching her old mother's hard heart.

Two weeks after this event the old blind woman suddenly appeared at the door of her daughter's house. This had never happened before. Imagine the daughter's surprise at seeing her old mother at the door! A little girl from the village had led her to the house. On arriving she dropped the little girl's hand and told her that she might return. The daughter wondered what this meant, but asked no questions, and set about making her mother comfortable.

At last the mother said: "Daughter, I have come to you to stay with you and to be what you are."

The previous night the old woman had dreamt that she was dying and that she passed on to the next world in company with her three children, two sons and the daughter referred to, who were all Christians. They walked up a lane lined with beautiful palms and flowering trees. At last they arrived at a broad gate, through which she got glimpses of a beautiful garden and people walking about. Her children were all in front of her as they entered. Then suddenly, a tall dark man with a long bamboo stick in his hand steped in front of her and stopped her. She asked him, "Why do you stop me?" "You do not belong here," he replied. "But my children, why do you part me from them, I will go where they go," she said, but the man told her that her children belonged there and that she must go away. Her children went on and joined the people within the gates and were lost to her sight, and she was turned back.

The dream was so vivid and real to her, that as she awoke, she sat up in bed and cried at the thought of being parted forever from her children. Her hard heart was melted, and she resolved then and there to break away from her heathen friends and the "Bonga" worship and become a Christian.

Together with a class of about twenty souls she was baptized on a Sunday morning. She not only answered the usual questions put to the candidates, but she interrupted the solemn proceedings by making quite a long speech to the congregation, setting forth the reasons for the step she was about to take and deploring the fact that she had waited so long before she accepted the invitation to come to her Saviour.

For half a year she lived with her daughter, and she used her time well. If she was unable to get someone to take her about to her old friends and relatives in the villages, she would send for them and entreat them earnestly to leave thir "Bongas" and come to Christ. When at last she was taken sick with dysentery, she told everyone that she was going to leave them. She knew she was going home. She died peacefully rejoicing in her Saviour. When no longer able to speak, she lifted her hand and pointed upwards.

From out of the darkness the Lord had led her into his own marvelous light.

BRINGING FIBRE GRASS TO MARKET.

GLIMPSES BEYOND THE VEIL.

Pandu was one of our Christian workers. He was not conspicuous for his brilliancy either as a preacher or as a catechist, but in his humble, quiet way, he bore witness for his master of the hope that was in him. Perhaps he was best known as the husband of Solma, the leading bible woman in this part of the mission field.

One day in the beginning of the rainy season, Pandu very suddenly passed away. His case looked like cholera, but there was no struggle, the end came quietly, and his last hours were full of joy and peace.

His wife told us that during the last month before he died he would often drop hints to the effect that his end was near. During the week before he died he spent his spare moments in making a new bed. One evening while watching him at his work, his wife made the remark that she thought that this bed would not be as pretty as some of the others he had made, for Pandu was rather clever with his hands and could make nice things. On hearing this remark he stopped working , turned to his wife and said in a quiet way: "I havn't the time to make this one pretty, as I shall need it very soon, for on this bed I shall sleep my last sleep."

His words came true; four days later he was carried to his last resting place on that very bed.

Bhima was a pupil in our boy's boarding school; he was about fifteen years of age when he died. He was the son of one of our preachers and brought up in a Christian home. From early childhood he had been taught how to pray and what it means to live a Christian life. At the age of eight he came to the boarding school. Although he did not distinguish himself as a scholar, yet with his true Christian character he won the love and esteem of both teachers and fellow-pupils. It is told of him, that when asked by an older boy to get some peppers from the garden of one of the teachers, who happened to be away from home that day, that young Bhima looked at the tempter and replied, "Do you think I will sell my soul to Satan for a pepper?"

About a month before Bhima died he called his special friend or chum aside and told him, that he soon would have to leave this world. "It will come about in this way," he said, "first I will get a headache and then two days afterwards I shall die. But I want you to promise me that as long as I am alive, you do not tell anyone what I have told you now. If my mother should find out that I am to die, she would feel very bad, so don't tell anyone."

Bhimas words came true. He took to bed one day with a severe headache. His chum was at his bedside and wept, for he knew what this sickness meant. "O Bhima, why are you going to leave me-" cried his chum. Bhima replied: "I am going on before you a little while. In three months you will join me and we shall be together forever."

Two days afterwards Bhima passed away trusting in his Saviour.

When Bhima's chum saw, that everything his friend had said about himself, came true, he became frightened and ran away from school. But like Noah's dove finding no place to rest, he returned, sought out Bhima's mother and told her everything. He was taken back into school again and three months later, precisely as Bhima had foretold,

WOOD SELLER.

he passed away to be with his friend, where there is no more parting.

Among a class of catechumens that were baptized in the Sohor district there was a nine year old boy by the name of Ram. For some time he had been suffering from fever and enlargement of the spleen and was quite emaciated. He was therefore not able to go to the pond to be baptized publicly like the rest of the class, but received the holy rite in his room, lying on his bed.

One day about a month after his baptism Ram was walking about feeling much better. His mother said, "You will soon be quite well again." To this He replied, "Yes, mother, I shall be better soon for I am going away tonight." His mother, thinking he intended to go to some of his friends, remarked, that she thought he had better wait a few days until he got stronger.

Across the street from Ram's home, Lutu, the Chrisian worker, who had been his instructor, lived. In Lutu's house all the Christians in the village used to gather for evening prayers. Quite early in the afternoon the boy began to ask for Lutu, saying, that he wanted him to gather the people for evening prayers. His mother told him that Lutu was out in the villages preaching, and would not return before dusk, and besides it was not yet time for evening prayers. But the boy would not be quieted, he wanted to have evening prayers right away. He went to the houses of all the Christians in the village and asked as many as he could find to come with him to evening prayers, as he called it. Nearly all the people were at their work in the fields, only children were at home, but these he gathered in the usual place and had prayers with them.

After prayers in which he had committed both himself and his playmates into the loving care of his Saviour, he told them plainly that he was to leave them. Several of the children went home weeping.

Lutu returned from his work a little earlier than usual. The children told him what had happened, and he went to the sick boy and found him lying on his bed, but very cheerful and contented. Lutu said: "What is it I hear about you? You are surely not going to leave us."

"Yes, uncle, tonight I am going," was Ram's reply.

"Why should you leave us now" said Lutu, "you have been getting much better of late and the Lord will surely make you quite well again and you will live to serve Him for many years."

But the boy repeated that he was going, and that he was only waiting for the messengers to come for him.

Lutu then sat down on the bed beside the boy and talked to him about Jesus and his heavenly home, and when the time came for the people to gather for evening prayers Ram folded his little hands, closed his eyes, and a little sigh told that the messengers had arrived, and the little spirit was free. Ram had been a Christian only a month.

In the village of Kaerabani there lived, some years ago, an old woman by the name of Lukhi. She was a quiet, unobstructive old soul, very fond of her grand-children and always to be found with one or two of them by her side in church on a Sunday.

Her oldest grand-daughter was about to be married. The banns had been published and the wedding day fixed. No one looked forward to the event with greater pleasure than the grandmother. But two weeks before the wedding was to take place she was suddenly taken ill with dysentery. In two days she became so weak, that she could hardly move in bed and all hope for her recovery was given up. The bride-to-be sat by her bed and wept saying: "O grandmother, why are you going to leave us, at least wait untill after my wedding, but don't leave us now."

"It will be as He wills," was the whispered reply.

Late in the evening she became unconscious, her feet and hands were quite cold and everyone thought she was dying. In this state she remained the most of the night. The family and other friends watched by her bedside. At dawn she opened her eyes, looked about her in a bewildered way and asked: "Where am I?" On seeing her granddaughter she said: "O, there you are. I am not going just yet. I will be with you and partake in your wedding feast."

She then told those about her what had happened to her. She had, as she expressed it, been to the other world and there she walked up a beautiful street, entirely different from anything she had ever seen. There were a lot of people about and they all looked so happy. From out of a group of children little Lukhi, one of her grand-children who had died the year before, came out and greeted her. But just then a tall man came up to her and in a pleasant voice told her that she would have to go back for a while yet. "In a month from now," he said, "you may return."

She then asked for some food and after a little while got up, dressed and took her broom and started to sweep the courtyard, as was her habit every morning.

She was quite well again and able to partake in the wedding festivities, and as she had foretold one month afterwards she passed away very quietly never to return.

REMARKABLE ANSWERS TO PRAYER.

The Santal Christians believe that God hears their prayers. They believe that if God has promised a thing, it must be so. He can not lie. When they see that Christ has promised: "Ask, and it shall be given you," — they believe that He who gave the promise is both willing and able to fulfill it. With childlike faith they lay hold of the promises and they are not disappointed.

At a meeting of the Christian workers the other day we were discussing prayer, and one of the men told us the following incident:

"Last week my youngest daughter, a child about five years old, was taken very ill. Little lumps, about the size of a bean, were raised all over her body and she suffered awfully. Although I have treated people for sickness and given medicine for years, I have never seen such a case, and several of the brethern, whom I called, also told me that they had never seen a case like this one.

We tried every remedy we could think of, but the child only grew worse. For three days and nights her mother and I watched by her bedside and prayed that our dear one might not be taken from us. On the fourth night we saw that she was growing very weak and we feared that the end was near. It was after midnight when I went outside and again cried to God to spare my child. After I had prayed a calm came over me. I did not worry any longer. God's will would be done. I entered the sick-chamber again, sat down on the mat beside the child's bed, leaned my head on the edge of the bed and in this position I fell asleep.

In a dream an old man came to me and asked me if I had faith in God. Three times he asked me this question, and each time I replied that I had. He then told me to put dust on the body of the sick child in the name of Jesus Christ and the child would live. When I awoke the day was just beginning to break. I took the moaning child in my arms, carried her out, put her on the ground and rubbed dust all over her body, the way the old man had told me. Then I put her on the bed again and she fell asleep quietly and slept for about two hours, when she awoke and told us that she was hungry. The child was perfectly well. The little lumps on her body were all gone. God had heard my prayer and in this wonderful way healed my child."

Another incident happened in our Girls' Boarding School a few days ago. One of the rules of the school had been broken. No one confessed, but suspicion fastened itself on little Muni, a nine year old girl, because she had committed that very same offence once before, and was then let off with a warning. The matron thought that this time she would have to take her punishment and proceeded to give her a little spanking.

Muni knew she was innocent and that she had been punished for the offence of another girl, and she felt the indignity very keenly. But the school bell rang and she wiped her tears and went to her class. At noon she refused to eat her dinner, but went to her sleeping-room, spread her mat, knelt down, and with tears told her Heavenly Father all about her troubles. One of the nurses sitting close by heard everything she said. She asked her

SANTAL FLUTE PLAYERS.

Savior to show her in a dream who it was that should have had the punishment.

Muni now lay down on her mat and fell asleep. When she awoke, about an hour later, she went to the matron and said: "Now I know who committed the offence for which I was punished. It was Manjhan."

"How do you know it was Manjhan?" the matron asked.

Muni then told her that she had asked Jesus to show her in a dream who the offender was, and that she had seen Manjhan. The nurse, who heard her pray, told the matron what she said in her prayer. Manjhan was then called and confessed that she was the guilty one. She asked Muni's forgiveness for the pain and disgrace she had caused her.

But I must tell you about Dumni, and how the Lord heard her prayer. Dumni had been given to us when she was a little girl six or seven years old. Her widowed mother was a heathen and very poor. There was famine in the district and many people suffered. Dumni's mother had one single hen which laid one egg a day. This egg little Dumni would bring to the mission every day and sell it, and for the money her mother would buy a little rice, from which she made soup for herself and her children. She had several sons, but Dumni was her only daughter. When the widow saw that she could not support all her children any longer, she brought Dumni to the mission and asked the missionary's wife to take her and keep her as her own child. The gift was accepted and shortly afterwards Dumni was sent to the Girls' Boarding School.

A few weeks ago she was confirmed together with a class of thirteen girls. On Monday previous to the confirmation Sunday one of the older girls in the school missed some money from her box, and accused Dumni of having taken it. But she pleaded her innocence and said she knew nothing about the money. The case was looked into, and, although there was no direct evidence that Dumni had taken the money, yet they were not able to clear her from the suspicion. She knew, that unless the case was cleared up and her innocence established, she could not be confirmed together with her class.

In her distress Dumni fasted and prayed. She also asked the other members of her class to help her in prayer. Every day the class met for Bible study and prayed. Saturday the last meeting was held, and up to then nothing had happened; the case was not cleared up.

The meeting was over. Final instruction for the morrow was given. At last Dumni was called and asked to confess, if she were guilty, and admonished not to forfeit her peace and joy for the sake of a few cents. But she answered that she could not confess that in which she was not guilty. With tears streaming down her face she said:

Every day I have prayed that God would clear up this matter, so that my innocence might be established, but until now He has not heard me. No one else can help me."

She cried as if her heart was breaking and her classmates were also crying. Just then the matron from the school arrived and announced that the case was cleared up, the money had been found, and that Dumni was innocent.

There was a moments pause, then Dumni said: Let us thank God." And she poured out her heart in thanksgiving and praise to God for her wonderful deliverance. She also prayed for the girl that had accused her falsely.

SAM, THE MEDICINE-MAN.

The subject of this sketch was born in a village called Ketosori in the Santal country. While yet a boy, Sam often had visions and wonderful dreams. When he was about nine years of age, an old man came to him in a dream and told him not to eat anything that had been prepared as an offering to any of the bongas; neither should he eat anything unclean, such as the flesh of animals that had died from disease.

For four years he kept this commandment. Then it happened that one of his neighbors was taken sick. An Ojha was called in, and after he had given the customary offerings to the gods, and medicines to the man, he recovered. After his recovery, a thanks-offering, consisting of cakes made from chicken and pastry, was given. These cakes were given to the relatives and neighbors of the man who was healed.

On this occasion, Sam was asked to take some of the cakes out to three or four boys who were herding cattle outside the village. On his way out, it occurred to him that he might taste one of the cakes. He was alone, so no one would be the wiser if he took one single cake. The temptation was too strong for him, and he fell. When he

SAM, THE MEDICINE-MAN.

had eaten the cake, he noticed that a large mango-tree by the way-side began to shake as if moved by a strong wind.

But it was a calm day. The boy stopped, and looked at the tree and wondered what this could mean, when suddenly a large branch was broken off and fell with a crash to the ground. Then he remembered his dream and that he had broken the commandment that the old man had given him. He became so frightened that he got fever and was sick for a couple of weeks.

During his illness, an old Ojha from the neighborhood attended him. When Sam told him about the tree, he explained to him that a bonga was after him and was trying to harm him. This fear caught the whole family and they decided to move away from the village. Consequently they gathered their possessions and moved eastward to the Sohor country and settled in a village about six miles west of the Ganges.

In this neighborhood there was an old medicine-man, who had a large number of "chelas" or disciples. Sam went to this man and soon became one of his most promising boys. When he had learned all the old Ojha had to teach him, he graduated at the Dasae festival. Together with their teacher, the class went from village to village. They sang and danced for the people and in turns went into trances, or were possessed by some bonga. After each performance of this kind, they begged corn from the people. Each boy gave his teacher a rupee and a goat, as pay for the pains he had taken in teaching him.

Sam also visited all the greatest medicine-men in the district and learned all he could from them, so that although he was but a young man he soon became a famous Ojha, not only among his own people, but also among the Hindus and Mohammedans. From near and far people sought him when they were sick or troubled by their bongas. They did not come empty-handed, but brought with them offerings of money, goats, pigs, fowls, and above all, plenty of rice-beer, so that Sam could indulge in the luxury of going to bed drunk almost every evening.

Several years passed by. Sam was married and had a family. One day two of his children were taken sick with dysentery. He gave them medicine and offered sacrifices

A CLASS OF YOUNG MEDICINE-MEN AT THE DASAE DANCE.

to the gods for their recovery, but they grew worse. After he had tried all the remedies at his disposal, and offered the largest sacrifices he thought the gods could demand without it having the desired effect, he went to a Hindu mendicant, or holy man, and asked him to make sacrifices to his gods for the children. He arrived at the shrine of the holy man early in the morning and the first thing he was asked after having stated his case was if he had eaten anything that morning. He answered in the negative and the holy man said:

"Very well, go to the Ganges and fetch a bottle of water. Buy some nuts, some butter, milkcurds, and vermilion in the bazaar and when you return we shall make an offering to the gods for your children. But take care that you taste neither food nor water before you return."

Sam was accompanied by one of his brothers. They went to the Ganges, a distance of four miles, and procured the things required by the holy man. It was in the month of May and the weather was very hot. They were both faint from thirst and hunger, when they returned. The holy man offered to his gods and assured Sam that his children would be saved. With hope in their hearts, they returned to their home, where they arrived late in the afternoon, but to their great disappointment found the children worse than they were in the morning. That night one of them died. The next night the other one passed away.

Then Sam said, "Now I am through with the bongas. I have offered the greatest sacrifices for my children and yet they did not make them well. They have evidently no power to heal. I shall never offer to them any more, no matter what happens to me, and I shall have nothing to do with them."

When Sam broke up his altar, people thought he was crazy and warned him not to do it, for if he did, the bongas would surely kill him.

Several weeks passed by, and nothing happened to Sam. People came to him as before to be helped. He gave them medicine which he prepared from roots and herbs, but performed no sacrifices for them. He was convinced that the bongas were false but that somewhere there must be a true God and he hoped to know him.

One evening in the rainy season, a young Santal came to his house, and asked if he could get lodging there over night. He was welcomed and shown genuine Santal hospitality. The young man was one of the village school teachers of our mission and had come to Sohor in connection with a law-suit. He was certainly led by the Lord to Sam's house. After the evening meal, Sam gave him a mat and showed him where he could spend the night. The young teacher spread his mat, sat down on it, got a book from his bundle and began to sing. The song was about the love of God and his care for those who trust in him. Sam's heart was touched. He had never heard the gospel of salvation before. All he knew about Christianity was that it was the religion of the white people and that some Santals had disgraced themselves by adopting it and were consequently outcasted. When the song was ended, Sam asked the young man to sing it again. This he did and then explained the song verse by verse. Neither Sam nor his guest went to bed that night. The young teacher told the old, old story of Jesus and his love over and over again.

For a whole month this young teacher stayed with Sam and instructed him and his family in the word of God. Then he came to the mission and asked us to send a catechist over to prepare them for baptism.

The Sohor country is outside of our missionfield, but the society working in that district had done no work among the Santals and were willing that we should baptize them. Consequently after they had been instructed, a pastor was sent over to baptize them.

After Sam and his family had become Christians, their

heathen neighbors would have nothing to do with them. They refused to give them fire, or to lend them anything, or help them when they were in need. Sam had very little land and was not used to hard work and it was not long before he and his family began to suffer want.

One evening he found his wife weeping. She told him that there was no food in the house and that everybody she had asked refused to lend her anything. Perhaps after all they had been foolish in becoming Christians. The outlook was very gloomy, but Sam took his troubles to the Throne of Grace and asked for help.

That night he had a dream or, perhaps, it was more like a vision. He saw a European standing on a high embankment directing a great number of people who were busy carrying earth on to the embankment beside a great river. Sam was made to understand that he should go to the white man and ask for work.

When the vision had passed away he understood that he should go to the Ganges where they were building a new rail-road just then. In the morning he told his wife that he was going away to get work. She said, "How can I let you go without getting any breakfast. Wait a bit and I will ask your sister again to lend us a bowl full of rice."

In a little while she returned with a little rice. This she cooked and gave him, and he was soon on his way to the Ganges.

Arriving at the river, he saw a great number of people at work building up an earthwork for a railway. Long lines of coolies carried earth in baskets on their heads and dumped it on the embankments. Among the coolies, directing their work, he saw a European and at once recognized him as the man he had seen in the vision. He went up to him, greeted him respectfully and asked him for work.

The European asked him if he could read and write. To this he answered in the affirmative and was told that he would get work at once directing a squad of twenty coolies. Besides his salary he would get a certain percentage of every square yard of earth his squad excavated. Sam was happy and with his heart full of praise to God he com-

SAM'S HOUSE AND CLASS OF CATECHUMENS.

menced his work. He sent for his family and lived in the camp for several months. Soon his squad was increased. At times he had as many as one hundred coolies working under him.

When the work on the railroad was finished, he returned to his village, paid all his debts and had enough left to live on for the rest of the year.

All this time he had been reading his testament and his knowledge of Christian truth increased. The trials he had gone through had deepened his spiritual life. He now began to speak to his friends and relatives in the neighborhood, inviting them to come to the Savior. At first they ridiculed him and asked him to mind his own business and leave them alone. Every day Sam cried to God for help that His kingdom might come to the Sohor country where so many of his people sat in darkness.

Across the street from Sam's house, his oldest sister and her family lived. This sister was a very strong opponent of Christianity and used every opportunity to thwart him in his efforts to win souls for Christ. But Sam prayed and waited for his opportunity and it came.

One of the sons of this sister, a lad of twelve years, was working for a Hindu in the next village. An unknown disease broke out in that village and several people died. One night two Hindus brought the Santal boy home to his mother's house on a stretcher. He was very ill. His throat was choking and he was unable to talk. The whole family was greatly alarmed and feared that the boy would die. In her agony, the mother ran across the street to her brother Sam's house, roused him and asked him to come over and, if possible, to do something to save her boy. Sam replied that of himself he could do nothing. It was not in his power to save the boy's life, but if she would give her heart to God and pray for her son, perhaps it might please God to show her mercy and heal her boy. She replied, "Yes, brother, I will believe in the God you believe in, but come quickly, and pray for my boy.

Sam soon knelt by the cot of the sick boy, placed his hands on his head and prayed that God should be merciful and save the boy so that the heathen might see that he alone was the true God.

After the prayer the boy sat up and took some ginger-water they had prepared for him. The next morning he was perfectly well. A few months later, he came to the

DURGA AND RARIA ON THEIR WEDDING DAY.

Boarding School for boys at Kaerabani and is a promising lad.

This occurance opened the eyes, not only of the friends and relatives of the family, but of the neighbors as well. They had seen with their own eyes that a boy, who was at death's door, had been healed through prayer. The God of the Christians must be the true God and stronger than their bongas.

From this time, people began to listen to the word of God. Their eyes and hearts were opened and soon a large number asked to be instructed for baptism. A few months later, Sam had the pleasure of seeing his first class of catechumens baptized. In all there were forty souls.

In the work of instructing this class as well as to shepherd them afterwards, Sam has been ably assisted by Durga and his splendid wife Raria, a graduate of our Girl's School at Benagaria. Shortly after their marriage, they were sent to Sohor to assist in the upbuilding of God's kingdom there.

THE VILLAGE POTTER.

THE SANTAL MISSION
OF THE NORTHERN CHURCHES.

The Santal mission, as it is commonly called, was founded in the year 1867 by two men, whose names are household words among the Scandinavian Lutherans, Boerresen and Skrefsrud.

H. P. Boerresen was a native of Denmark, born in the city of Copenhagen, Nov. 29, 1825. His parents were poor laboring people and his chances to acquire an education were very limited. He learned the trade of a mechanic in his native city and when about 27 years of age he went to Berlin, in Germany, to learn mechanical engineering and to better his conditions.

It was while he was yet a stranger in Berlin that he heard his Savior's voice calling him and he received grace to believe that his sins were forgiven. He soon began to take part in the religious activities of that city and thus came into contact with people who were interested in missions. Among others, he became acquainted with Mr. Hempel, whose daughter, Caroline, later became his wife.

The marriage took place in the summer of the year

H. P. BOERRESEN.

1855. Both Boerresen and his young wife were interested in missions and felt called to offer themselves as workers in heathen lands. Their desire was to go to China, but no way was opened for them and several years passed. They had to be led through sorrow and trials before they were ready to say: "Lord, where thou leadest we will follow!"

L. O. Skrefsrud was born in Gudbrandsdalen, Norway, Febr. 4, 1840. His parents were very poor and the family was a large one. They were in all 9 brothers and sisters. His father was a shiftless man and the family often suffered want. His mother was a warmhearted Christian woman who took all her troubles to God in prayer.

While yet a lad in his teens, Skrefsrud had to leave home and shift for himself. He worked for some time in a machine shop at Lillehammer and it was his desire to keep his confirmation vows and the promises he had given his mother on his departure from home. He had been away from home a little over a year, when he received the sad news that his mother was dead. This was a hard shock to the young man for he loved her dearly and felt that he had lost his best earthly friend.

A year later he joined a highland regiment as drummer boy, fell into bad company, forgot his vows and lived a Godless life. But his mother's prayers should not remain unanswered. His sins found him out and he had to suffer bitter consequences. He was awakened to see his awful condition and after long struggles found peace with God.

Simultaneous with his conversion the desire of becoming a missionary to the heathen was kindled in his heart. He began to study, especially languages, and to prepare himself for the lifework before him. At this time he lived in Christiania, the capital city of Norway. He had no money to spend for schooling but worked all day and

L. O. Skrefsrud

studied in the evenings, receiving help now and then from students at the university in the city.

In 1863 Skrefsrud applied for admission at the training school for missionaries, shortly before established in Stavanger, but was refused. This was a great disappointment to him and to ease his heart he told his troubles to a Christian friend, Mr. Holte. This man advised him to go to Germany and seek admission to one of the training schools there. Holte also told him that one of his sons had just returned from Berlin and could give him directions about the journey and perhaps also give him letters of introduction to Christian friends in that city.

Skrefsrud sought young Holte, got the desired directions about the journey and a letter of introduction to Mr. and Mrs. H. P. Boerresen in Berlin.

Skrefsrud arrived in Berlin, in the fall of 1862, and found the Boerresens, who were destined to become his friends and coworkers as long as he lived.

For one year Skrefsrud attended the Prochnow Mission School and on his graduation he received a call from the Goszner Society to join their mission to the Coles in Chota Nagpur, India. Before he left Berlin it was agreed that Boerresen and family should come out and join him as soon as they had disposed of their business.

In May 1865 the Boerresens joined Skrefsrud at the mission station Purulia. It was a joyful meeting, but their joy was not to last long. A disagreement arose between the German and Scandinavian missionaries and the latter resigned their service as missionaries in the Goszner society. Through trials and difficulties the Lord led them His own way to the glory of His name.

From Purulia they returned to Calcutta, where Christ-

SKREFSRUD, MR. AND MRS. BOERRESEN.

ian friends assisted them, and the Lord soon had them where He wished to use them, among the Santals.

A September morning in 1867 these two servants of God gathered a few stones south of the village of Benagaria in Santal Parganas where they had received some land from a Bengali landlord, called it their Ebenezer and kneeling consecrated themselves anew to God and to his service among the Santals.

They had no mission society and no funds to fall back on, but trusted in God that He would provide for them, and they were not disappointed. Boerresen had to spend a good deal of his time the first years in traveling about in India soliciting funds for the mission. Skrefsrud threw all his energy into the study of Santali, and so great were his abilities as a linguist, that after three years he published a Santali grammar which after having stood the test for over forty years, is still the standard work in that language.

On the 28th of March 1869 they had the great joy of baptizing three young men, the first fruit of their labor among the Santals. Forty-four years have passed since that joyfull event. They have been years of trials, struggles and tribulations, but also years of glorious victories When Boerresen on the 21st of September 1901 was called home to his rest not only a Christian community of 13,000 souls but even the heathen Santals, Hindus and Mohammedans, who had come in contact with his great, warm heart, mourned his departure.

On December 11th, 1910 when Skrefsrud passed away after an illness of nearly two years the Santal church had a membership of over 15,000 souls.

At the time of writing this little historical sketch the membership has risen to about 17,000, and the work is growing a steady and healthy growth.

It was the hope of the founders of the mission that the funds for its support should be raised in India, therefore they called it "The Indian Home Mission to the Santals." After Skrefsruds death the mission was reorganized and now bears the name found at the head of this chapter. It is supported by contributions from friends in Norway, Denmark and America. Each of these countries have a comittee which together with the trustees of the mission are responsible for the continuation of the work.

Until today the Lord has helped, and may we not rest assured that He will continue to help his servants until the last battle is won? For he is faithful that promised.